MULTICULTURAL EDUCATION SERIES

JAMES A. BANKS, *Series Editor*

(continued)

LGBTQ
YOUTH AND EDUCATION
POLICIES AND PRACTICES

DISCARD

Cris Mayo

Teachers College, Columbia University
New York and London

Published by Teachers College Press, 1234 Amsterdam Avenue, New York, NY 10027

Library of Congress Cataloging-in-Publication Data available at www.loc.gov.

ISBN 978-0-8077-5488-7 (paper)
ISBN 978-0-8077-5489-4 (hardcover)
eISBN 978-0-8077-7244-7 (ebook)

Printed on acid-free paper
Manufactured in the United States of America

21 20 19 18 17 16 15 14   8 7 6 5 4 3 2 1

Contents

Series Foreword

Identity-safe classrooms promote the academic and social success of students by recognizing, legitimizing, and validating their personal, cultural, and community experiences (Steele, 2012; Steele & Cohn-Vargas, 2013). In this informative, insightful, and needed book, Cris Mayo describes in powerful and sometimes poignant ways how schools and classrooms are not "safe" environments for Lesbian, Gay, Bisexual, Transgender, and Questioning (LGBTQ) youth. The hostile environments that LGBTQ youth experience in their homes, schools, and communities result in many negative consequences, including higher rates of depression, suicide, dropout rates, and more academic challenges than students who are perceived as heterosexual. However, while Mayo describes the problems that LGBTQ youth experience in society and school throughout this sobering, compassionate, and skillfully crafted book, she chronicles the problems that result when LGBTQ youth are portrayed only as victims and not as resilient individuals who have agency and who can and do act to influence their destinies. Mayo advocates striving for a balanced view of LGBTQ youth that describes their problems but that also depicts them as individuals with agency and resiliency.

An important message that is evident on nearly every page of this incisive and discerning book is that in order for educators to create identity-safe classrooms for LGBTQ youth and their allies, they must transform their thinking about gender, gender identity, sexual orientation, and race in order to understand how these concepts are complex, interactive, and interrelated. There are several important reasons why this book is appropriately published in the Multicultural Education Series. One is that Cris Mayo thoughtfully discusses how variables such as race, social class, and sexual orientation interact and intersect to influence the behavior of youth. Important goals of multicultural education are to create identity-safe classrooms for all students as well as to create classrooms and schools that promote social justice. As Mayo makes clear throughout this original and timely book, an important aim of schools should be to create environments that promote social justice and caring for LGBTQ students as well as for all students.

When classrooms and schools become safe environments for LGBTQ students and promote social justice for them, all students will benefit and flourish, including the large number of immigrant students who are now populating the nation's schools. Students whose first language is not English is the fastest-growing population in U.S. schools. The 2010 American Community Survey indicates that approximately 19.8% of the school-age population spoke a language at home other than English in 2010 (U.S. Census Bureau, 2010).

American classrooms are experiencing the largest influx of immigrant students since the beginning of the 20th century. Almost 14 million new immigrants—documented and undocumented—settled in the United States in the years from 2000 to 2010. Less than 10% came from nations in Europe. Most came from Mexico, nations in Asia, and nations in Latin America, the Caribbean, and Central America (Comarota, 2011). A large but undetermined number of undocumented immigrants enter the United States each year. The U.S. Department of Homeland Security (2010) estimated that in January 2010 10.8 million undocumented immigrants were living in the United States, which was a decrease from the estimated 11.8 million that resided in the United States in January 2007. In 2007, approximately 3.2 million children and young adults were among the 11.8 million undocumented immigrants in the United States, most of whom grew up in the this country (Perez, 2011). The influence of an increasingly ethnically diverse population on U.S. schools, colleges, and universities is and will continue to be enormous.

The major purpose of the Multicultural Education Series is to provide preservice educators, practicing educators, graduate students, scholars, and policymakers with an interrelated and comprehensive set of books that summarizes and analyzes important research, theory, and practice related to the education of ethnic, racial, cultural, and linguistic groups in the United States and the education of mainstream students about diversity. The dimensions of multicultural education, developed by Banks (2004) and described in the *Handbook of Research on Multicultural Education, The Routledge International Companion to Multicultural Education* (Banks, 2009), and in the *Encyclopedia of Diversity in Education* (Banks, 2012), provide the conceptual framework for the development of the publications in the Series. They are content integration, the knowledge construction process, prejudice reduction, an equity pedagogy, and an empowering institutional culture and social structure.

The books in the Series provide research, theoretical, and practical knowledge about the behaviors and learning characteristics of students of color, language minority students, low-income students, and other minoritized population groups, such as LGBTQ youth. They also provide knowledge about ways to improve academic achievement and race relations in educational settings. Multicultural education is consequently as important for middle-class White suburban students as it is for students of color who live in the inner city. Multicultural education fosters the public good and the overarching goals of the commonwealth.

In this significant and informative book, Mayo focuses on the plight, challenges, and possibilities of one of the most neglected and marginalized group of students in our schools. As she makes explicit in this book, LGBTQ students are within all racial, ethnic, cultural, linguistic, and religious groups. Consequently, dealing effectively with the challenges and possibilities of LGBTQ youth will benefit all segments of the nation's school population. In addition to describing the challenges that LGBTQ youth experience in society and in schools, Mayo describes how educators can transform their thinking in ways that will enable them to respond creatively and effectively to the problems of LGBTQ youth and to construct educational interventions that that will create identity-safe schools and classrooms for LGBTQ youth as well as for all students.

—James A. Banks

REFERENCES

Banks, J. A. (2004). Multicultural education: Historical development, dimensions, and practice. In J. A. Banks & C. A. M. Banks (Eds.). *Handbook of research on multicultural education* (2nd ed., pp. 3–29). San Francisco, CA: Jossey-Bass.

Banks, J. A. (Ed.). (2009). *The Routledge international companion to multicultural education.* New York, NY and London, UK: Routledge.

Banks, J. A. (2012). Multicultural education: Dimensions of. In J. A. Banks (Ed). *Encyclopedia of diversity in education* (Vol. 3, pp. 1538–1547). Thousand Oaks, CA: Sage Publications.

Camarota, S. A. (2011, October). *A record-setting decade of immigration: 2000 to 2010.* Washintgton, DC: Center for Immigration Studies. Available at http://cis.org/2000-2010-record-setting-decade-of-immigration

Perez, W. (2011). *Americans by heart: Undocumented Latino students and the promise of higher education.* New York, NY: Teachers College Press.

Steele, D. M. (2012). Identity-safe environments, creating. In J. A. Banks (Ed.), *Encyclopedia of diversity in education* (Vol. 2, pp. 1125–1128). Thousand Oaks, CA: Sage Publications.

Steele, D. M. & Cohn-Vargas, B. (2013). *Identity safe classrooms: Places to belong and learn.* Thousand Oaks, CA: Corwin.

U.S. Census Bureau. (2010). *2010 American community survey.* Available at http://factfinder2.census.gov/faces/tableservices/jsf/pages/productview.xhtml?pid=ACS_10_1YR_S1603&prodType=table

U.S. Department of Homeland Security. (2010, February). *Estimates of the unauthorized immigrant population residing in the United States: January 2010.* Available at http://www.dhs.gov/files/statistics/immigration.shtm

Acknowledgments

It is hard to adequately acknowledge the help I have had in teaching, thinking, and writing on LGBTQ youth or to even adequately chart the changes in terminology and patterns of association that have complicated the subject. As a young lesbian, just coming out, my grandmother set the stage for all the complexities to come by telling me the story of her friends Bill and Pearl, who lived together in a small upstate New York town in the decades before I was born. The story began, "Do you know about Bill and Pearl? Well, Bill's name was Camille, of course." She recounted that they had lived together for decades and Bill, not exactly passing as a man but certainly not dressing as a woman, worked at the newspaper and would always take kids from town who couldn't otherwise afford it into Buffalo to baseball. My grandmother ended the reminiscence with an indication that I didn't need to worry and that she'd always wanted to be a gym teacher. Then we went out to dinner with my Aunt Margaret who was living with Pearl by then.

I am grateful to the gay student group and other queer, bisexual, and straight youth I met while at the University of Delaware, visiting student groups in Salt Lake City, Toronto, small town Ohio and small urban Illinois who, generously shared their experiences of homophobia, racism, and sexism and who also showed what student resistances can do to improve communities. Butch, sissyboy, genderqueer, and transgender youth, whether in organized school groups or not, have also generously discussed the complexities of gender that they live in schools and elsewhere. Stacey Gross and Billy Vaughn, both teachers who organized Gay-Straight Alliances have helped me to meet another generation of student activists and to begin to understand how teachers, too, negotiate institutional constraints and possibilities. Discussions of all these topics have been enhanced by students in my Sexualities and Education seminar and the organizers of the University of Illinois at Urbana-Champaign College of Education yearly event, the Rainbow Bookbag, which offers sessions for local teachers on LGBTQ issues. Michael Parrish, Johnell Bentz, Bryan Lake, Leslie Morrow, Saida Bonifield, Rae Montague, Lucas McKeever, Anita Hund, and the late Sue Noffke, among others, have shown what a small group of energetic people can do to help an even larger group of committed teachers improve practices. I am also grateful to colleagues in LGBTQ studies who worked across disciplines to improve our work in the social sciences and humanities: Megan Paceley, Liz Holman, Joe Robinson, and Ramona Oswald. Thanks also to Scott Richardson and Louis Bergonzi for inviting me to give talks based on earlier versions of these chapters and providing me with wonderful audiences with which to engage. I owe a debt of enormous gratitude to Zelia Gregoriou, Carren Pacuyan, and the students at the University Cyprus, as well as my colleagues Megan Boler, and Eugene Matusov for their help with the development of parts of this book.

Thanks, too, to James Banks for his help in ensuring inclusion of LGBT issues into multiculturalism and his encouragement on this project. I am grateful to Xiuying Cai's help in collecting some of the sources for this book. In addition, I am grateful for conversations with her and other graduate students, including Chris Cayari, Ga Young Chung, Tanya Diaz-Kozlowski, Tony Laing, Debra Larson, and Norma Marrun for insights that have helped shape my thinking. Thanks to discussions on these and related topics with Stephanie Foote, Audrey Thompson, Erin Castro, A. Finn Enke, Frank Galarte, Pat Gill, Heather Greenhalgh-Spencer, Scott Gust, Kim Hackford-Peer, Nancy Kendall, Natasha Levinson, Jennifer Logue, Vicki Mahaffey, Lisa Patrick, Carmen Ocon, Wanda Pillow, Chad Prosen, Barbara Stengel, Lisa Weems, and Tom Zook this work is much improved. Thanks, too, to my mother, Jane Franck, now retired from teaching, whose model of supportive educator is much in evidence in vast array of students and parents with whom she stays in close contact. Earlier plans for this book were greatly influenced by Nelson Rodriguez's brilliance. The final form of this work would not have been possible without the close reading and incisive critiques from Stephanie Foote and Audrey Thompson (all shortcomings are my own) and the keen eye of copy editors at Teachers College Press.

Finally, without the quotidian joys, the dog pack life, and spectacular kayaking with Stephanie Foote, nothing would ever get done or be worth it.

Introduction

This book examines the pedagogical, curricular, and policy changes that can improve school experiences of LGBTQ (lesbian, gay, bisexual, transgender, queer) and ally students.[1] In so doing it tries to balance the challenges of discrimination, harassment, and alienation that LGBTQ students and their allies face with their creativity in organizing against those challenges as well as their resilience. It is itself a challenge to avoid positioning LGBTQ youth as only victims or completely able to fend for themselves. Negative school-based experiences, including those that encourage LGBTQ students to drop out of school, lead them to substance abuse, and harass them into disproportionate rates of suicide or thoughts of suicide, are all issues that teachers and administrators need to be aware of as they make curricular and policy decisions and as they interact with students on a daily basis. At the same time that institutions need to take responsibility for forms of hostility and exclusion they may engender, LGBTQ students and communities need to be understood beyond the lens of victimization. LGBTQ communities are vibrant and resilient, and have long histories of resisting homophobia and transphobia and also have long histories of doing much more than defensive work. They meet one another, form social networks, achieve school success, and do all the sorts of things many young people do. Supportive political and educational networks are as close as friends, the Internet, community center, or organizations, both formal and informal, that are started by LGBTQ students in school. Likewise, LGBTQ parents and teachers create supportive resources for themselves to help them negotiate school exclusions. Allies, too, are often present to join in the struggle for equity on the basis of sexual orientation and gender identity, aware that such changes also benefit people of all sexualities and genders. Nonetheless, schools need to do more to respond to sexual identity and gender identity diversity. The purpose of this book is to show why it is important that teachers, administrators, and other members of the school community provide support for LGBTQ students and advocate for changes to current school practices in order to improve LGBTQ student experiences and outcomes. Such support helps show that LGBTQ families and school professionals are seen as contributing members of the school community.

---

1. I will use LGBTQ to include a wide range of gender and sexual minorities. Many of the authors cited in this text use LGBT or LGB to refer to their research subjects so any variation in usage reflects those differences.

This kind of educationally based advocacy needs to be undertaken with a complicated understanding of LGBTQ youth, adult, and community experience, attentive to how differences in gender, race, ethnicity, class, region, and gender identity, as well as ally status, enable students to share some but not all experiences of what it might mean to be LGBTQ in school. Racial and class segregation in public schools, for instance, helps shape racial and class segregation in LGBTQ youth communities and organizations, and experiences of racism or classism may affect students more than homophobia or may prevent cross-racial or cross-class alliance around sexuality-related issues. The intersection of racism and homophobia and/or transphobia, too, exacerbates LGBTQ youth of color experiences of bias. Gender and gender identity, as well as racial and ethnic differences, also affect the array of harassment experienced by LGBTQ youth and subsequently affects school attendance and completion more. Without attending to the specificity of intersectional identities, attempts to improve school climate for LGBTQ students may replicate racial, class, and gendered divisions among LGBTQ students. LGBTQ faculty, staff, administrators, parents, and other family members also add complexity to how we might think about the relationship of LGBTQ issues and education. Further, it is important in all work on LGBTQ-related issues to be clear that racism, sexism, genderism, ablebodism, ethnocentrism, and classism, as well as prejudice against religious people, are all concerns that LGBTQ people need to attend to, not only because it's simply ethically right to do so but also because the LGBTQ communities represent such diversity.

Attention to intersectionality—how racialization affects sexual identity, gender, social class, and gender identity, for instance—complicates the commonsensical if mistaken ideas about homogeneous experiences among, and educational needs of, LGBTQ students. There are also commonalities that youth face when dealing with the heterosexism and homophobic environment in schools, but because sexuality is understood as raced, classed, gendered and so on, the particular experiences may vary. LGBTQ youth of color, for instance, report higher incidents of physical violence (Diaz & Kosciw, 2009) and note that White LGBTQ students' racism keeps them away from school-based programs to help sexual and gender minority students (McCready, 2010). Studies of LGBTQ youth experience differ on whether young men or young women experience more harassment. On the one hand, normative masculinity, or what R. W. Connell called "hegemonic masculinity," seems to have less flexibility than femininity (Connell, 1987). On the other hand, the Human Rights Watch report (Bochenek & Brown, 2001) on homophobia in schools found that the interlinked experience of sexual harassment and homophobia and the isolation of gender-nonconforming young butches seemed more extreme than that of other LGBTQ youth. Then again, genders are relational categories that exceed the norms of male and female so beginning to tease apart which gender has a worse experience being harassed into normativity not only overly dichoto-mizes gender, it sets up a hierarchy of injury that would be impossible to calcu-late. The simpler point is to improve school experiences for diverse students. In order to enable school community members to begin to address these and other interlocked issues in a productive way, this book includes strategies for pedagogy, curricular revisions, and policies that have had positive effects on the school experience of LGBTQ youth, as well as changed schools for the bet-ter for all students.

Attention to LGBTQ issues may raise difficult challenges for schools trying to address the needs and concerns of parents and students from diverse back-grounds. This book includes discussions of controversies that have been raised over curricular changes, additions to nondiscrimination policies to include sexual orientation and gender identity, as well as challenges to improving the experiences of LGBTQ youth and their allies, as well as all students, in public schools. I hope these sections will help thoughtful practitioners understand the challenges involved in creating schools that serve LGBTQ students and fami-lies well and also understand why it is that some parents and religious groups object to doing so. My intention is to provide strategies that open discussions and aim at constructive engagement that encourages respect for all, but also remains committed to improving the school experiences of LGBTQ youth.

Drawing on queer theory, gender studies, multicultural theory, educational policy, and youth studies, it is my hope that discussions will be useful in a broad array of education, interdisciplinary, and gender-studies related courses and contexts. This book consists of six chapters, each of which will provide historical, theoretical, and practical grounding for preservice education stu-dents, teachers, and administrators to use to help develop a more complex understanding of gender identity and sexual orientation, and the ways that each are part of how everyone learns and lives. While the text addresses the challenges facing educators who want to make schools more responsive to gen-der and sexual minorities, there are also indications throughout that schools are addressing such concerns and that change is possible even if issues around sexuality and gender identity remain difficult and complex. Throughout its various chapters, this book explains how interventions can improve outcomes for LGBTQ students and improve the work lives of LGBTQ faculty, adminis-trators, staff, and family members. Innovative projects, curricula, and policy changes have begun to have positive effects on LGBTQ learning, aspirations, and school climate.

This chapter introduces key policies for supporting LGBTQ and ally youth, as well as acknowledging the controversies that surround any attempt to educate about sexuality and youth, especially LGBTQ sexuality. Chapter 1 provides a variety of ways to situate the history and contemporary movements for LGBTQ rights, showing intersections among sexual orientation, gender identity, race, gender, class, and ethnicity, as well as giving definitions for key terms related to gender and sexual diversity. Chapter 2 examines the process of gender and how school-based practices reinforce its salience or keep definitions of gender in play, noting as well the relationship between gender and sexuality and other intersections. The links between homophobia and transphobia, as well as the possibilities for new queer relations among terms of identity are also discussed. Chapter 3 details the specific obstacles LGBTQ youth and their allies face in schools and suggests that "bullying" is a term that is insufficient to meet the institutional constraints that cause or exacerbate school-based exclusions. Chapter 4 advocates for a more complex pedagogical approach to LGBTQ issues in schools, highlighting both the disruptions of queer pedagogy and examining a variety of discipline-based approaches to teaching students to think about LGBTQ-related concerns. Chapter 5 shows how young people have helped improve school climate for LGBTQ youth and allies, by organizing into extracurricular groups or creating school-based and community-based interventions. Chapter 6 highlights the role of online communities and web-based resources for youth understanding of sexual and gender minority issues.

NECESSARY TENSIONS

Schools often contribute to the silencing of sexual minority students and to the subtle support for harassment and even violence against LGBTQ students. The history of education, taken up in the next chapter, shows that schools have long been flashpoints for controversies over sexuality. More recently, schools and educational policymakers have been involved in efforts to have LGBTQ teachers fired or prohibited and put limitations on sexuality and HIV education, and they have neglected to protect students from anti-LGBTQ bias. Still, schools have also mounted efforts to include LGBTQ issues in various subject areas and extracurricular activities in schools, tried to be better at accommodating LGBTQ parents, and helped provide employment protections for LGBTQ school employees. This chapter will provide students with the policy and legal context for understanding how LGBTQ issues have been used symbolically in larger cultural and political debates.

Research on and advocacy for LGBTQ students sometimes runs into an impasse. Should LGBTQ students' experience of bullying and exclusion take center stage or should the ability of LGBTQ students to negotiate, resist, and create new possibilities for alliance and community be the primary focus? If we only discuss LGBTQ students as at-risk, we position sexual and gender minority students as victims and potentially neglect how they work their way through institutions that may not protect them from discrimination, represent them in curriculum, or encourage schools to make all facilities available to them equitably. If we emphasize how much LGBTQ students are able to accomplish, showing that they are their own best advocates, that their energies to ensure that all students have an opportunity to learn about LGBTQ history and politics, that gay and lesbian students can bring their partners to prom, that transgender students have access to choose the bathroom that fits their chosen gender and the ability to choose their own names, and so on, it may appear that there is little left to be reformed in schools. Thinking about how and when students identify as queer, questioning, ally, straight, transgender, lesbian, gay, and/or bisexual, or terms that get closer to the more individualized ways they feel like genderqueer (intentionally disrupting the meanings of gender) or pansexual (rejecting gender as a category defining attraction) or those understandings of identity that either take multiple, seemingly contradictory labels or refuse labels altogether. Students, too, insist on particular kinds of recognition and outness, some of which take advantage of the kinds of networks they create and so trying to negotiate with them about when and where they want to be known is a complex process.

As a tactic of analysis, taking the middle road and saying that LGBTQ students are somewhere between resilient and victimized can also be a problematic approach. By indicating that the other sides in any debate are extremes, the middle road gets to claim a kind of superior, disinterested balance. My interest in this book is to highlight both the restrictive school climate and the energies of those who are working to improve it in order to show the tensions between emergent possibilities and pervasive restrictions. As anyone working in or with schools knows, schools are sites of institutional forms of repression and also places where policies and practices enable change. It is important, too, to see that LGBTQ youth can reflect and rework the forms of gender and sexuality resistance that energized the LGBTQ movements and communities that came before them, but to also see where youth take LGBTQ communities and movements from here. They live, like we all do, in a context of possibility and constraint. Social institutions that used to explicitly exclude LGBTQ people are increasingly inclusive, but not, by any stretch of the imagination, completely so. The military may no longer prohibit lesbians and gay men from service, but it continues to exclude transpeople. Same-sex or gay marriage is legal in thirteen states (a number I have revised multiple times while writing this book) but prohibited by state constitutions in three-dozen states. But the social context of such laws is seemingly ever-changing so even indicating which state allows what is tricky: Nothing dates a book on LGBTQ issues more than an attempt to give current laws and regulations on the topic. Perhaps, too, nothing erases the long work done by gay movements than now referring to gay marriage as "same-sex marriage." At the same time, concentrating only on marriage-related political reform misses many of the critiques of gender roles, economic inequality, racism, and sexuality-related state regulations that early LGBTQ movements addressed. Further, even marriage-related reforms are not yet equal, sweeping, or fully inclusive. The Supreme Court ruled to allow federal benefits for same-sex married couples and returned the question of Proposition 8 to California, thus relegalizing same-sex marriage there, but the patchwork of laws regulating transpeople's participation in marriage is still complex, dependent not only on whether same-sex marriage is legal (in some cases) but also on whether states' allow gender of choice to be on official documents (American Civil Liberties Union [ACLU], 2013b). In addition, the Supreme Court's ruling on federal marriage benefits and Proposition 8, while full of supportive language about same-sex marriage, did not go so far as to indicate that marriage is a right protected by the Constitution, thus leaving many gay and lesbian couples still unable to access marriage rights, federal benefits, or even, in the event of the dissolution of their partnership valid in a same-sex-marriage state, a way to get divorced (Goode, 2013). The federal government, for now, has shown willingness to open immigration to binational gay and lesbian couples married in states that recognize same-sex marriage but living in states that do not (Preston, 2013). It is unclear whether such policies will become practice in another administration, however. Lesbian, gay, and bisexual people are covered under laws that prohibit discrimination based on sexual orientation, and in some states those laws include gender identity (ACLU, 2013a). In other cases, gender identity may be a protected class using Title XI, not sexual orientation protection (ACLU, 2013b). For LGBTQ people of color, racism, too, continues to shape their experiences and policies enacting racial or ethnic equality may be of more immediate importance to their key concerns. Even when laws and policies protect against discrimination, of course, discrimination can still happen. And, to follow the argument that stresses resilience, even when people live under discriminatory laws, they can still flourish, build resistant communities, and even avoid experiences of prejudice and bias, if they are able to make choices about the company they keep.

Students cannot always make those choices, and so even if they are able to be active in improving their school climate, the practices of schools precedes their involvement in it. Experiencing LGBT-related bias at schools is associated with negative outcomes, including lower attendance rates, lower grade point averages, and a lower sense of connection to school (O'Shaughnessy, Russell, Heck, Calhoun, & Laub, 2004; Poteat & Espelage, 2007). Gay and lesbian students also experience isolation from heterosexual peers (Poteat & Espelage, 2007). In addition, experiences of school-based bias can lead to negative health outcomes including depression, substance abuse, and suicidal thoughts (Williams, Connolly, Pepler, & Craig, 2005). Transgender students experience bias against their gender nonconformity at school and at home (Grossman & D'Augelli, 2006). The negative school-based experiences of transyouth may not be improved by programs aimed at LGB students so schools need to understand and teach about transgender-related issues specifically (McGuire, Anderson, Toomey, & Russell, 2010). In addition, as will be reinforced throughout this book, sexuality and gender–related bias can be experienced by LGBTQ students, their allies, or youth who are perceived to be LGBTQ, and further, the effects of this bias spreads to the entire school community.

But teachers and administrators are in a unique position to ensure that their schools and districts have a working discrimination policy that includes sexual orientation and gender identity. Further, school officials, teachers, and staff can ensure that the policy is itself part of the educational experience of all students and that all students are able to access an equitable and safe educational environment. All education should be challenging and even difficult, but providing for physical and emotional safety from oppression, bullying, and microaggressions can help all students learn. When biases are challenged as not educative—and educational information about forms of discrimination and why they are unethical is part of education—all students are invited to participate in the school community and all students learn. In addition, school personnel can be open to the work that LGBTQ youth and allies are doing to improve school and community experiences for all students, and respond with support for such youth-based interventions. In examining laws and policies that support an equitable school, I am not only suggesting that schools follow the rules, I am also suggesting that we understand any law or policy as itself the beginnings of education. Policies, laws, and legal decisions begin to teach us how to get along and with more educative curricula and pedagogies, all of these educational strategies are especially useful for pushing schools to be equitable places of sexual and gender minorities and their allies. But we also need to remember that policies gesture toward possibility: they do not fill in all that might happen or all that people might become.

LAYERS OF RESPONSIBILITY AND PROFESSIONAL SOURCES FOR JUSTIFICATION FOR NONDISCRIMINATION

Teachers and administrators ought to care about students in ways that go beyond what laws, policies, and professional codes require. Most educational professionals, hopefully, do work beyond the basic requirements set up by such policies and rules because they understand that teaching well requires caring about students. But understanding professional obligations and being able to communicate those to other professionals and community members may be a helpful way to start school-based conversations about LGBTQ students, allies, parents, and their rights and hopes for education. The simplest point may be that if a school professional wants to be an advocate for all students, including

LGBTQ students, that person is not alone: Professional standards for each level of authority in schools includes nondiscrimination policies and legal rulings that make it clear such policies need to be put into effect. However, as I will discuss later, policies and laws communicate expectations, but if people do not know about them or do not put them into effect, they do not have their fullest intended and educative impact. The most basic protection that all members of the school community have is that the Constitution guarantees equal protection of the laws and freedom of speech, whether or not there are state or local laws protecting LGBTQ people in particular. In addition and more specifically, Title IX of the Education Amendments of 1972 protects students from gender discrimination in educational programs or schools that receive federal funding. Understanding that most schools are already obligated to provide such protections may help educators ensure that their schools are compliant. But understanding that LGBTQ issues are not settled in the broader communities may seem to be an impediment for doing so.

Teachers and administrators who want to make their school safer for all students may be concerned that raising the issue of anti-LGBTQ harassment and violence will put them at odds with other school professionals, their school board, or community members. But understanding that those who are involved with schools are already obligated to do so may make advocacy easier. Even in areas that have protections for LGBTQ people, including same-sex marriage, educators may find opposition to LGBTQ teachers or curricular inclusion. Carrie Kilman (2012) reports the analysis of an lesbian educator in Massachusetts, reflecting on the growth of opposition to gay teachers after her state legalized same-sex marriage in 2003:

> "Once a group gets a little power, people maybe become a little more afraid," Howe says. "The fact that marriage was legitimate made the people who were politically against having out teachers become more adamant and active."

While varieties of legal protection do enable change, policies and laws need to be explicated as well as put into practice, and understanding how opposition to both may take place will also help engage broader community discussions.

Beginning conversations about LGBTQ students in light of laws and responsibilities may be a way to remind school authorities that they have access to resources and should be interested in proactively avoiding legal problems associated with discrimination. School board members may already know that the National School Boards Association (NSBA) can be a resource for them and can help them strategize how to communicate the need for districts to have firm and inclusive nondiscrimination policies. The NSBA provides guidance on laws and suggestions for practices that ensure nondiscrimination of LGBT youth, including information on school district and private liability in cases where school personnel did nothing to stop peer-to-peer harassment. Knowing that inattention to bias and harassment can lead to significant monetary settlements or to federally directed consent decrees may help motivate districts not only to have policies in place but to ensure that they are followed. The 1999 Supreme Court decision in *Davis v. Monroe County Board of Education* found that school boards could be held responsible for private damages in the case of student-on-student harassment if such authorities were deliberately indifferent. In Davis's case, the 5th-grade girl and her mother repeatedly asked various teachers and the school principal to intervene in the intense and repeated sexual harassment she was experiencing from a boy in her class but nothing was done. Her grades dropped and she considered suicide. The Supreme Court ruled that the administrator's and teachers' indifference to her and other students' complaints created the kind of hostile environment prohibited by Title IX. If school authorities remained indifferent to student complaints, the court ruled, they could be held liable and sued for damages and discrimination.

In another Supreme Court case, *Oncale v. Sundowner Offshore Services, Inc.* (1998), a case involving a man sexually harassed by another man, the Supreme Court ruled that same-sex sexual harassment was a violation of Title VII of the Civil Rights Act of 1964. Subsequent court decisions have also included same-sex sexual harassment as prohibited by Title IX. The federal appeals case that provided some of the basis of this Supreme Court decision was directly concerned with homophobic violence in schools. In *Nabozny v. Podlesny* (1996), a district court held school officials responsible for their indifference to same-sex homophobic assault and harassment, so severe that Jamie Nabozny required surgery to stop internal bleeding. Despite multiple complaints to teachers and administrators, Nabozny was told he should expect such treatment because he was gay. School officials did nothing to prevent the continued abuse over a number of months. Just before it was to go to a jury to determine financial liability, the case was settled out of court by the school district, which agreed to pay $900,000 to Nabozny. When the Supreme Court ruled in *Davis v. Monroe* and established private liability for school officials who neglected to intervene in gender-based hostile environments, the National School Boards Association (NSBA) sent a pamphlet on the issue to every school board in the United States, indicating not only invention in gender-based, sexualized harassment was a best practice but also that it would be costly to not intervene. In addition, the NSBA recommended that districts include sexual orientation in their nondiscrimination policies, not only because they are committed to see that all students are respected in schools but also because such proactive efforts to provide support for LGBTQ students can help schools plan for any response to homophobic harassment and violence they might encounter.

The largest teachers' union in the United States, the National Education Association (NEA), also includes a nondiscrimination policy as part of its professional code of ethics:

> In fulfillment of the obligation to the student, the educator . . . 4. Shall make reasonable effort to protect the student from conditions harmful to learning or to health and safety. 5. Shall not intentionally expose the student to embarrassment or disparagement. 6. Shall not on the basis of race, color, creed, sex, national origin, marital status, political or religious beliefs, family, social or cultural background, or sexual orientation, unfairly a. Exclude any student from participation in any program, b. Deny benefits to any student, c. Grant any advantage to any student. (NEA, 1975)

The NEA and the American Federation of Teachers (AFT) have had caucuses in their respective organizations for decades, each advocating for job protections for LGBTQ teachers and school professionals, as well as attention to the education-related impact of other LGBTQ-related laws and legislation. In addition, the NEA also advocates for the rights of LGBTQ teachers through its Advisory Committee on Sexual Orientation and Gender Identification. Because there is no federal-level nondiscrimination policy that includes sexual orientation and gender identity, teachers across the United States are subject to a variety of different levels of employment protection. Currently, 19 states offer no such protections and only 16 include both sexual orientation and gender identity as protected classes (Human Rights Campaign, 2013).

NSBA, AFT, and the NEA, among other groups, also offer workshops and materials on how to make schools accessible to transgender students, including information on restroom equality, gym classes, and athletics, and ensuring access to education by addressing potential bullying and bias. Understanding how existing school laws on gender provides resources for protecting the rights of transgender youth not only encourages an understanding of the links among forms of diversity, but also may help members of the school community more fully understand how gender operates—and potentially excludes—within schools (Jacobs, 2013). Bringing new attention to gender segregation even in schools that are attempting to be gender equitable can restart critical conversations about what gender means and who gets to decide. In addition, ensuring that students can choose their preferred names and pronouns not only shows that a school community understands gender diversity, it shows a willingness to be responsive to students' needs and identities. Further, attention to the forms of bias students experience from other students via "bullying" (which now appears to be used as a catchall term for everything from teasing to violence) and institution-based exclusions—like gender "appropriate" dress and restroom use—can open the conversation about how exclusions operate on multiple levels. Understanding that there are resources available and that schools and districts have been able to make positive changes may help even LGBTQ-supportive school professionals who are concerned that their local communities would not be open to such reforms.

According to Lambda Legal, a legal resource for LGBTQ communities, "laws are a floor, not a ceiling. Schools can and should do more than the legal minimum to ensure safety and equal education for transgender students" (Lambda Legal, 2008). They suggest taking the Los Angeles Unified School District as a model for comprehensive policies on transgender students, including allowing students to make their own pronoun and name choices, giving them access to restrooms and locker rooms conforming to their gender identity or allowing them alternative spaces, and ensuring that they are protected from discrimination and that their transgender identity is kept private, except to those who need to know because of their professional responsibilities (Lambda Legal, 2008). Because student gender identity is recorded on official school records, any information about it is covered by the Family Educational Rights and Privacy Act (FERPA) and cannot be released without consent.

STUDENTS' RIGHTS TO EXPRESSION, PRIVACY, AND ASSOCIATION

In his book *The Right to Be Out: Sexual Orientation and Gender Identity in America's Public Schools*, Stuart Biegel (2010) argues that the right to be out as LGBT and be an ally is protected by the Constitution and that being able to be public about one's identity is crucial to full participation in education. LGBTQ students are protected by the First Amendment and the series of decisions that come from *Tinker v. Des Moines Independent Community School District* (1969), a Supreme Court decision that ruled that schools cannot limit student or teacher expression without serious concerns that the discipline of the school will be disrupted. Speech and expression can be unpopular or controversial and still be protected, a point reinforced in *Fricke v. Lynch* (1980), in which a district court ruled that a Rhode Island principal could not forbid a gay couple to attend the prom based on his concern that because one of the young men had already experienced harassment and violence at school because of his sexuality, other students would be intolerant at the prom as well.

More recently, in 2010 in Mississippi, Constance McMillen asked the ACLU to intercede with her school and the court because she was first forbidden by the school to attend prom with her girlfriend and forbidden, as well, to wear her tuxedo to the prom. Initially, the school cancelled the prom, and then, in response to a negotiation with a judge and the ACLU, seemed to reinstate the prom and allow McMillen to wear her tuxedo and bring her female date. It turned out that there was a prom organized at a local country club for almost all the school's students, but McMillen, other gay and lesbian students, and students with learning disabilities were invited to and attended a "fake prom" in another location. She has since won $35,000 in damages, the school has agreed to be held liable for violating her rights, and the district has been ordered to have a nondiscrimination policy that includes sexual orientation and gender identity (Esseks, 2010). The machinations of the school district are notable not only for their duplicity but also for their apparent decision to make a number of students official outcasts, showing that harassment and bias extend beyond sexuality and that taking on issues one at time, whether sexual orientation, gender identity, or other forms of exclusion like learning disabilities, is an insufficient strategy. McMillen has since worked to lobby for a federal law that would prohibit public school discrimination against students based on "actual or perceived sexual orientation or gender identity" (Thompson, 2010).

Harassment and discrimination based on sexual orientation and gender identity, as is evident from the wording in the proposed federal act, happen to students of all sexual orientations and gender identities, including heterosexual-identified students who act as allies to LGBTQ students. Heather Gillman, a heterosexual-identified student, came to the aid of one of her friends, a lesbian who had been harassed by other students, and was threatened with being outed to her parents by the school principal. Gillman and other allies of the lesbian student decided to wear T-shirts and buttons in support of gay rights. In response, the principal, whose well-known anti-gay opinions had been expressed to the lesbian student and Gillman's gay cousin, also a student, threatened Gillman with punishment for organizing a gay rights group. The principal had already suspended her cousin. As a result of that suspension, Gillman wanted, with other concerned students, to indicate support for gay rights in school by again wearing T-shirts. Having already been cautioned by the principal for her political advocacy, Gillman contacted the school board for clarification of what she could wear to school. The board agreed with the principal that the following legends on T-shirts and buttons were impermissible:

> "Equal, Not Special Rights," "Gay? Fine By Me," "Gay Pride" or "GP," "I Support My Gay Friends," "I Support Gays," "God Loves Me Just the Way I Am," "I'm Straight, But I Vote Pro-Gay," "I Support Equal Marriage Rights," "Pro-Gay Marriage," "Sexual Orientation is Not a Choice. Religion, However, Is." (*Gillman v. School Board of Holmes County*, 2008, p. 5)

The district court ruled in favor of Gillman and chastised the principal for his behavior toward the harassed lesbian student; because the school board provided no justification for prohibiting Gillman's expression, they were both liable for ensuring that no further discrimination on the basis of homosexuality continued.

Biegel (2010) argues that the right to be out in schools includes the ability to determine when and where to be out. Citing the case of *Nguon v. Wolf* (2007), he provides an example of a district court judge who ruled that students have "a Constitutionally protected privacy right with respect to disclosure of . . . sexual orientation" (p. 33). Charlene Nguon had been disciplined by the principal of her school for violating the school rules against public displays of affection, and in notifying her parents about why she was being punished, the principal explained that she had been engaged in such public displays of affection with another young woman. The ruling found the school had acted correctly and had disciplined both heterosexual and gay students for breaking the rule and, in addition, had an obligation to inform the parents of the reason their daughter was disciplined—for public display of affection with her girlfriend. In his discussion of the case, Holning Lau (2007) argues that the court understood Nguon's right to privacy and could have made a balanced decision that both protected her parents' right to know why she was punished and her right to maintain privacy with them. While Nguon was out at school, Lau argues, young people ought to have the ability to maintain privacy rights in ways that recognize their particular need to develop identities. Schools should not disclose sexual orientation or gender identity to parents if the student does not want that information shared because, Lau argues, "the developmental state of childhood renders children particularly vulnerable to the harmful effects of assimilation demands" (p. 318).

Part of learning about identity can involve learning in community with others, whether of the same identity category or supportive of that identity. Gay-Straight Alliances are one such supportive and diverse social context in which LGBTQ and ally youth can work and learn together (Miceli, 2005). The federal Equal Access Act (EAA) of 1984 requires that any school that is a "limited open forum"—allowing noncurricular groups to meet—must also allow even potentially controversial groups, including LGBTQ-related groups such as Gay-Straight Alliances (GSAs) space as well. Designed to protect the right of religious students to form extracurricular groups at schools, the EAA has helped a wide variety of student groups use school space to develop their interests. According to the Gay, Lesbian & Straight Education Network (GLSEN), which keeps track of them, there are over four thousand GSAs in the United States (GLSEN, 2013a), and most have met with success using the EAA as their justification even in seemingly unsupportive communities. However, a number of strategies to discourage GSAs have also been used, a point I will return to in more detail in Chapter 5. Some states now require parental notification or parental permission before a student can join an extracurricular group, essentially requiring students to out themselves, whether as LGBTQ or LGBTQ-supportive, to their parents if they want to participate in a GSA. In addition, districts that require an abstinence-only curriculum have also used such curricular restrictions as an indication of community values and as a justification to deny GSAs to organize (Mayo, 2008).

PREPARING TEACHERS AND LEADERS TO BE ADVOCATES

Like any other segment of the population, preservice teachers come into their education with prejudices and biases that need to be identified and challenged before they enter schools as professional teachers. Preservice teachers, perhaps because they simply do not know about LGBTQ youth and culture or because they are resistant to thinking about sexual and gender diversity, are especially in need of more concerted education about their own effects on students and the pressures of institutionalized heteronormativity (DePalma & Atkinson, 2006; Ferfolja & Robinson, 2004; Wyatt, Oswalt, White, & Peterson, 2008). Analysis of teacher education programs also point to the need for more robust attention to other areas of diversity as well, including, race, ethnicity, language, and religion. Because this book takes an intersectional approach to thinking about LGBTQ students—examining how sexual orientation and gender identity are one aspect of students' identities that also intersect with their other identity categories—bringing more attention to each one of these categories of diversity will also help diverse LGBTQ students have access to education and flourish in schools.

Preparing teachers and school leaders to be advocates for all students means working against those prejudices that circulate widely and, further, making sure that school personnel learn about the ways schools as institutions exacerbate already existing divisions and biases. Because schools do more than teach basic subjects but also teach students how to become members of communities and part of the progress of the nation and the world, teachers, school leaders, school staff, and counselors all need to be prepared to work with diverse learners, community members, and parents, and to advocate for the equitable learning of all students. Learning about diverse histories and learning how to create an inclusive school community links the process of social justice with the process of education.

School leaders, like teachers, are increasingly responsible for ensuring that students learn up to the expected standards for each grade level. This intense attention to accountability has sometimes pushed teachers and administrators to get "back to the basics" without adequate attention to how access to education is impeded by experiences of bias. Offering what they call a "nonessentialized" version of social justice for school leaders, McKenzie et al. (2008) argue that school leaders need to be prepared to engage both the necessity of student accountability and learning and also attention to the difficult task of developing school-based social justice. Recognizing that pressures to prioritize accountability can be used to derail social justice education, they instead explain how critical consciousness and educational accountability are linked with an intersectional approach to social justice:

> We strongly recommend that they must know how to do all three tasks: to increase student achievement as evidenced, in part, by high test scores; to raise the critical consciousness among their students and staff; and to accomplish these tasks by creating intentional, heterogeneous learning communities for students and staff. Indeed, these social justice leaders must view high student achievement in the context of critical consciousness and inclusive communities as a disrupting and destabilizing intervention into the racist, classist, sexist, homophobic, and ableist education system in this country. (McKenzie et al., 2008, p. 117)

Anderson (1997) and Capper (1999) have pushed school leaders to analyze how assumptions about sexual orientation shape their leadership practice and their vision for schools, encouraging them to learn more about sexual orientation and how to respond more effectively to homophobia, as well as other biases. Capper (1999) has found that sexual-minority educational administration students were more concerned than other educational leadership students to ensure that students of all identities were able to access equitable education. They showed a willingness not only to address LGBTQ issues but also to be sure that all diversities found respect in schools. All administrators, of course, should aspire to leadership that encourages the full participation of all members of the school community and makes respectful learning part of their interlinked mission of educational accountability.

Studies and legal cases indicate that students and their parents do report harassment and find that administrators do not respond. The cases detailed above show that administrators and districts are liable for such neglect and that leaders need to ensure that their schools have policies that cover discrimination and that those policies are enforced. Blaming students for their experiences of homophobia is a commonplace and misguided response to such situations. Indeed, Capper, Schulte, and McKinney (2009) argue that such a response is, in effect, a re-victimization of students. Instead, they offer a comprehensive approach for school leaders, starting with inclusive nondiscrimination policies and ensuring that school leaders are publicly engaged in supporting those policies, as well as quick to intervene in bias-related activities. In addition, Capper et al. (2009) note that success against bullying is also related to proactive support for minority student organizations, like GSAs. The change to the school climate, in their experience, needs to come from the school leader and be responsive to students who also want to improve their schools. Communicating to the school board and community how and why such interventions need to take place, including concern for abstenteeism and learning outcomes, can help ensure that the reasons for developing respectful school communities are understood by more than just those who attend and work in schools. But as multiple authors caution, this respect cannot be a lukewarm version of tolerance or only a decision to address LGBTQ youth as at-risk students, who need to be protected either because they are helpless or because legal liability threatens the status quo. Schools, too, must move beyond the simple baseline requirements of federal, state, and local laws or professional codes to become spaces where all students can learn (Hackford-Peer, 2010; Lugg, 2003).

CHAPTER 1

Background to LGBTQ Movements for Equality with a Focus on K–12 Related Issues

Many education students, as well as teachers and administrators, may not be aware of the longer histories of sexual and gender minorities or the educational and school-related issues associated with gay rights movements or with the diversity of gay rights issues across race, class, gender, and gender identity. Tracing out different origins of political movements and communities built around sexual orientation and gender identity can help explore how such formations link up with different aspects of identity or mobilize different forms of critique. This chapter provides provisional definitions of key terms of identity related to LGBTQ peoples and communities and examines various historical and political starting points to discussions about the complexities of gender, sexuality, and other aspects of identity, community, and activity. The purpose is twofold: (1) to show how communities and identities organize in relationship to other aspects of difference, and (2) to show that opposition to sexual and gender minorities is also shaped in response to such intersectionalities.

By providing complex and diverse histories of sexual and gender minority people, I hope this section provides educators with a fuller contextual understanding of how various attempts to open cultural conversations about sexuality and gender were started, and sometimes repressed. The multiple histories and starting points for these discussions reinforce the point that sexuality is a complex issue. Some of the movements associated with sexual and gender minorities are well known, some are known but not always linked to sexuality and gender transgression, and others rarely make it into history lessons at all. But by tracing their various different starting points and different trajectories, it becomes apparent that any starting point for thinking about the subjects of sexual orientation and gender identity is just one option in a complex field of possibilities.

For many of the new generation of teachers, school leaders, and preservice education students, discussions of LGBTQ-related political and social issues are nothing new. Debates over same-sex marriage have had center stage in national politics for nearly 20 years. Increasingly, schools are responding to concerns about bullying, and a number of prominent national cases have involved anti-gay harassment and violence. What may be less familiar are the educational aspects of rethinking the cultural dominance of heterosexuality and challenging gender norms that not only pressure young people to be correctly gendered but limit gender expression of those for whom such dominant categories are insufficient. As the cultural climate changes and the rights of gender and sexual minorities are being recognized in state and federal laws, schools must find ways to respect those rights, to ensure that learning environments are not spaces of bullying, and to work so that curricula, school activities, and school facilities represent diverse sexualities, genders, and forms of relationship.

Schools need to not only include more respectful policies and representative curricular materials but also move beyond a simple process where lesbian, gay, bisexual, and transgender issues are added to what is already taught as if such lessons weren't already there, either not fully marked or as if LGBTQ people were not already in schools. Further, schools need to educate about LGBTQ issues because all people, no matter their identity, are actively involved in the processes of gender and sexuality negotiation themselves. An additive process misses the opportunity to examine how we all live within and exceed the normative or dominant conceptions of appropriate gender identity and sexual orientation. Simple additions, too, miss the place of gender identity and sexual orientation in wide varieties of histories. Attention to these complexities means taking into account how institutions and norms shape such understandings of gender identity and sexual orientation. There may be some approaches to multiculturalism and diversity education that seem to indicate that cultures are unchanging or that the biases that help structure institutions can be addressed without thinking about the norms of such institutions as themselves a problem. But these versions of diversity education are pale versions of the kind of transformative teaching, learning, and action that most multiculturalism, diversity and equity education, and social justice–related education aim toward. Rethinking education in light of sexual and gender diversity will change more than holidays that are celebrated and famous figures covered by curriculum, though adding some of that information or at least being more honest about diverse representation of sexuality and gender identity already in the curriculum can help.

Changes in cultural norms around sexuality and gender mean rethinking how we think about education, challenging the normalities that have structured schools, and helping facilitate the next generation of further changes to how sexuality, gender, gender identity, race, ethnicity, disability, religion, and other forms of diversity are thought, lived, and educated for. In most cases, teachers, administrators, school counselors and other members of the school community are committed to teaching all students, so considering what "all" students means in terms of sexual orientation and gender identity can help schools broaden their scope of address, the inclusiveness of their climate, and the effectiveness of their teaching.

Like the first time we think about forms of diversity we haven't considered before, the first response may be to wonder at how we've remained ignorant. Arguably, our knowledge is defined by and through our ignorance (Logue, 2008). Lessons and policies represent the interests of dominant members of any community and, through the decision to limit representation, can contribute to keeping minority identities and issues from students. In other words, ignorance is structured into curricular and policy decisions. This is a perennial problem for education, and certainly sexuality education is no exception in that regard. To begin to undo this ignorance, but also be cognizant of the processes by which all knowledge creates other ignorances, it is necessary to question the central categories by which educational institutions categorize and educate. In the midst of being critical of how certain sexual orientations and gender identities have come to be dominant and how others have worked to be recognized or organized, learners need to take stock of where they are, consider what they have systematically ignored or avoided, and begin to move to new considerations of the possibilities that have, at least to some extent, remained outside the regular curricula or outside the considerations of policy.

The introduction to this volume provided information on how rights and liability can help districts be more inclusive. This chapter examines how learning and knowing about sexual orientation and gender identity can alter our relationship to how we situate ourselves in relation to histories and movements and to how we think and learn. By examining what is persistently missing, we can also think about the most difficult thing about education: the process of taking stock of where we are now, what we ignore, and moving to somewhere else. In addition, we can think more about the limitations of narratives that read backward too simplistically. Inasmuch as the histories of sexuality and gender identity are complicated by race, gender, social class, and other issues, rethinking and resituating the beginnings of various movements and communities offers us resources for where we might go next, perhaps thinking about why we ignore so much of what has happened before and how we continue to structure our knowledge through ignorance and denial. To return to the disruptive function of the word "queer," even this project of rethinking and restarting sexualities and genders will inevitably be insufficient. Any account even of complex sexuality and gender identity will miss other potential narratives of origins and relationships and will miss, too, the ways that such stories over-stabilize the meanings and critiques implicit in diverse and dissident sexualities and gender identities.

KEY DEFINITIONS, OFTEN IN FLUX AND CONTESTED

Sexuality and gender identity are themselves complicated concepts, including both diversity of sexual partners, gendered bodies and identities, and other related categories of difference increasingly organized under the general term *queer*. *Lesbian*, *gay*, and *bisexual* may seem like relatively easy concepts to understand but even within those categories there may be cultural and regional differences, different relationships to normative gender identity, and differing degrees of politicization of sexual orientation. LGB people and, indeed, all the various sexual and gender minorities may decide to be out and open about their difference, decide to pass, or decide in different contexts to be out in different ways. Bisexual people may find it more challenging to be out when they are dating someone of another gender because they are assumed to be heterosexual. Anyone who is not actively working to be out and likely explaining themselves to others may be misrecognized as heterosexual or gender normative. *Heterosexism* and *heteronormativity*—the first, the assumption that heterosexuality is superior, and the second, the pervasive assumption that sexual and gender difference is just not there—are both social processes that make the assertion of sexual or gender difference difficult for all people, including those heterosexuals who are allies or do not themselves conform to social norms. I will refer more often to normativity (the process by which norms or standards are practiced or infused into institutions) in reference to norms of gender and sexuality, rather than specifically linking the process of instilling norms only to heterosexism.

Despite histories of common struggle for rights, different groups that may organize within the LGBTQ movement have different targets for their political action or different emphases on personal and community needs. For instance, *transgender* people—people for whom gender categories are insufficient to express their identities or people whose birth sex does not conform with their gender identity—may find some common cause with lesbian, gay, and bisexual (LGB) people but centralize gender identity above sexual orientation. *Gender transgression*—that is, activities meant to critique "normal" gender roles and expectations, including drag performances, and political activities, as well as non-normative gender identities such as genderqueer—have long been part of LGBTQ and queer culture, but LGBTQ movements have not maintained consistent attention to the challenges or transphobia or the different issues that transgender people face. *Cisgender* people, people whose gender identity and birth gender are the same, may take for granted the ease with which they negotiate gender norms, though they too can recall being corrected for not acting in properly gendered ways.

All sexual minorities may be very aware and critical of how gender norms constrain their lives, but for transgender people gender identity is a central site of political struggle. Some transpeople may use medical or other interventions in order to bring their bodies into conformity with their gender identity while other *genderqueer* transgender people may work to have their bodies and identities reflect gender complexity that moves beyond the normative binary of female or male. Transmen and transwomen, that is, transgender people who remain open about their transgender identity may also disrupt expectations that surgery, hormones, or crossdressing is done to assimilate to normative gender. *Bigender* young people, who maintain aspects of both male and female, as well as queering gender by so doing, also challenge how normative concepts of gender seem to keep male and female distinctively different and in different bodies. Transgender young people are making their gender identity known earlier and finding more support from school districts and parents, but social disapproval remains and attempts to protect the rights of transgender students have not yet found broad support.

Other people also concerned with the relationship between gender and normative bodies include intersex people. For *intersex* people—that is, people with bodies that are not easily categorized by dominant categories of male and female—medical intervention to "normalize" their bodies without their consent is a key political issue. Intersex and transgender activism reminds the medical establishment, parents, and the broader community that young people deserve to be able to give informed consent about an issue so crucial to self-identity as gender, as well as recognize that people will live beyond stable meanings of gender. These descriptions may themselves seem to stabilize what the various forms of gender and sexual identity mean and so they are better taken as a very brief summary of the vast diversity of gender and sexuality-related possibility. However complex people may be, however, normative expectations from people and institutions remain barriers to their creativity and innovation. Gender nonconforming people or people perceived to be gender nonconforming also experience transphobia and homophobia, like other people whose gender identity does not conform with the dominant norm.

The "Q" in LGBTQ usually refers to *queer* although it may also stand for *questioning*. Queer is a concept and identity that works against problematic forms of normalization, troubling the exclusions that any category of identity may enact. Because the processes of normalization and the pressure to conform to dominant understandings of gender and sexuality affect people of all sexual and gender identities—including heterosexual and conventionally gendered cisgendered people—examining the processes of normalization provides all people with a way to critically engage cultural, political, and educational messages about gender and sexuality. *Questioning* students, that is, students who are critically analyzing their sexual orientation, are reminders that the process of having a sexuality is just that: a process. Research indicates that for students who are questioning their sexuality, school is an unwelcoming place

(Birkett, Espelage, & Koenig, 2008; Russell, 2002). Questioning or even shifting attractions from one gender to another can also happen at any stage of life. Lisa Diamond and Ritch Savin-Williams (2000) analyze the shifts in same-sex attractions across women's life courses, showing that, for women, sexual attraction is not always related to their sexual identity.

A more complete acronym signaling concern for the broad links between people who organize around gender identity, gender expression, and sexual orientation community building and practices is LGBTQQICA—lesbian, gay, bisexual, transgender, queer, questioning, intersex, curious, ally—including both curious and ally people in the mix. Given concerns that each instantiation of movements and communities organized around gender identity or sexual orientation have created exclusions, ensuring that such exclusions are challenged is necessary. Being willing to be curious about other ways of being or interacting and being willing as well to ally with those with whom one does not share an identity or experience is a hopeful sign that when the subjects of gender and sexuality are opened, they are not too quickly closed into meanings already in circulation.

OPENING THE SUBJECT OF SEXUALITY AND GENDER THROUGH THEORY, HISTORY, AND POLITICAL MOVEMENTS

The complexity of sexuality and gender identity can be studied through psychology and other empirically based fields as well. Post-structural theory and social constructionism in sociology can help us think through sexuality critically, especially work from the early 1980s like Michel Foucault's (1980) work on institutional formations and resistances and Jeffrey Weeks's (1990) examination of the social processes, large and small, that provide the context for meaning-making, political formation, and all manner of restraint and freedom. Political writings, too, rooted in civil rights, feminism, and queer politics show a variety of different ways into thinking about sexuality and gender identity. Audre Lorde (1984, 1988) and the Combahee River Collective (1982), among others, insist on the necessity of fighting for justice by recognizing the interlocking ways race, gender, and sexuality shape meanings, lives, and possibilities. For them, any political movement that neglects any aspect of that complexity will ultimately fail. Others like Carl Wittman (1970) argue that gay men can teach heterosexuals and lesbians to appreciate sexuality more, but that gay men need to learn from people of color to take responsibility for race. Lesbian feminists like the Radicalesbians (1970) shift the category of lesbian into political critique of patriarchy and encourage all women to consider how they are kept from recognizing themselves and the value of other women as well. Each of these different approaches to political change push us to think about sexuality on a number of different scales and critically examine our foundational definitions of what counts as sexuality by resituating it in its political, raced, gendered, age-related, institutional, and personal contexts, among others.

To begin to undo the heteronormativity that seems to define sexuality, starting with Alfred Kinsey and associates' studies of sexuality can provide a reminder of complexity and the widespread effect of a study that showed such complexity in sexuality. The Kinsey scale, running from zero for exclusively heterosexual to six for exclusively homosexual, is a model that offsets the presumption of heteronormativity, showing that practice of sexuality is much more complicated than its norms. In his large-scale studies of male and female sexual behavior in the United States, Kinsey (Kinsey et al., 1948, 1953, respectively) found that most people do not exclusively identify as heterosexual or homosexual but instead fell somewhere in the middle of a continuum of both. Kinsey's work was a popular success as well as the first study of its kind and scale undertaken by a scientist. References to the Kinsey Report abounded in the popular culture of the time and while there are good reasons to think earlier generations were more sexually restrictive than contemporary times, given laws prohibiting abortion, contraception, and homosexuality, nonetheless, the popularity of Kinsey's work and its popular reception indicates a keen interest in finding out more about people's sexualities and understanding the broad array of sexual difference. At the same time that Kinsey's studies were fascinating the American reading public and his name and findings were sliding into popular songs and plays, the federal government was rooting out gay people from government work (D. K. Johnson, 2006). While schools may teach about McCarthyism and the Red Scare, less attention is given to the fact that the majority of people who lost their jobs in public service were gay men and lesbians rooted out in what is more accurately referred to as the Lavender Scare (D. K. Johnson, 2006). Fears that gay men and lesbians would be open to blackmail because of their sexuality or that their inherent perversity made them poor employees led to firings and forced resignations, often leading to years of unemployment or underemployment for highly educated professionals (D. K. Johnson, 2006).

A similar but longer history of concern about the normative gender and sexuality of public school teachers shows that a combination of gender bias, bias against married women, and suspicion of single women has also led to strict surveillance of teachers. Indeed, schools have long been institutions careful to ensure their employees were normatively gendered (Blount, 2006). During the McCarthy era and well after, schools, too, undertook concerted efforts to remove gay and lesbian teachers, or teachers suspected of being gay or lesbian (Graves, 2009). Teachers have long been caught in a double bind; fired if they were out at school or fired if they neglected to be honest about their sexuality on job applications (Sedgwick, 1990). At the same time that schools were known to be restricted to dominantly gendered and heterosexual employees, sexual and gender minorities were also teachers and administrators (Blount, 2006, Graves, 2009). By thinking about how the institutions are both discriminatory and inhabited by diverse people at the same time, even in time periods characterized by wide-scale legal repression, we may get a fuller sense of how resistance, interest, and oppression operate side by side.

Given the pressures of normativity, as Adrienne Rich (1980) and other feminists remind us, how do we even know our own desires, shaped as they are by restrictive definitions of gender and sexuality? Or, given Foucault's (1980) critique of how sexuality has come to signal the mistaken "freedom" of those desires, why do we keep asking without seeing how such efforts at liberation tie us more closely to a problematic subjectivity? How do we enact education and politics to welcome what comes next? To that end, it may help if we start with where we are and in the midst of so doing also move that place—where we think any conversation starts sets the terms for how it continues, and so thinking about histories with more complexity may help us keep moving toward educative possibilities.

OVERLAPPING HISTORIES OF LGBTQ MOVEMENTS

The modern gay liberation movement usually dates its beginning to a rebellion of bar patrons at the Stonewall Inn in Greenwich Village, New York, on June 28, 1969. Many of the protesters were young people of color and included lesbian, gay, and transgender people. After years of harassment by police, LGBTQ people decided to fight back, unleashing days of unrest in New York City and providing a center for the political organizing already begun there and elsewhere. However, dating the start of any movement is problematic; for instance, the 1966 Compton Cafeteria riots protesting the exclusion of gender nonconforming people from that establishment predate Stonewall and centralize the link between gender and gay liberation (Stryker, 2008). Other important dates and activities are also associated with the beginning of the LGBTQ civil rights movement. Smaller political advocacy groups or activists starting in the early 20th century challenged the categorization of homosexuality as a psychological disorder. Multiple small sexual and/or gender minority communities developed in various racial, ethnic, gendered, and geographical locations before Stonewall.

A different beginning could be in the discussion groups and organizations in various places at the start of the 20th century that thought about same-sex attraction as an indication of a third sex. Whether in Berlin or later in Chicago, such groups drew together people concerned with social restrictions placed on gender and sexual minorities and advocated for changes in law and social custom. Such formations highlight the relationship between gender and sexuality, and rather than trying to equate homosexuality with heterosexuality, they shift into new possibilities of being gendered. The early 20th century in New York City shows the start of urban subcultures of men identifying as fairies, adopting recognizable forms of dress, meeting in particular areas of public taverns, and socializing with each other as well as other men. George Chauncey's (1994) historical research on this potential origin story shows not only the development of ideas about the third sex but also the complex negotiation between public and private that fairies and their companions engaged in. Socializing in plain view, dressing distinctively, and being known publicly—yet also, for some, using pseudonyms or living apart from the fairy culture in order to maintain professional lives as well—shows that the idea of the closet has been oversimplified.

Pushing histories of same-sex attraction further back might get us to accepted practices of attraction, flirtation, and intense romantic relationships among women in the nineteenth century, before the rise of psychoanalysis made such intensities suspect (Faderman, 1981). School-based crushes between girlfriends and even the social acceptability of same-sex attraction to offset the potential for heterosexual romance shows both that young people have long been capable of expressing desire and that there is often a complex relationship between the heterosexual norm and same-sex desire (Sahli, 1979). Carroll Smith-Rosenberg's (1975) research on such intense female friendships also indicates that what began in school carried on throughout women's lives, with friends visiting one another, staying in close, intimate contact either in person or in letters. Like Chauncey's discussion of the beginnings of gay male urban culture, these histories of women's attractions for one another show the public place and recognition of such relations and indicate as well the social pressures to also conform to the expectations of married life.

Other ways to start a consideration of the place of gender and sexuality in creating communities and eventual change might shift from prior to mass political organizing and instead look at the beginnings of LGBTQ media. In the 1950s, at the same time that gays and lesbians were being fired from civil service and professional employment, small publications advocating for gay rights, like the *Mattachine Review,* and lesbian rights, like *The Ladder*, or sexual freedom and freedom of expression, like *ONE Magazine,* were finding a readership and helping organize the smaller political groups that were also advocating for change. Lesbians, gay men, and their allies wanted such publications to be ways to bridge distances between communities or ways for isolated LGBTQ people to find connection, much like the Web provides connection today. Publications, too, focused on helping LGBTQ people learn more about themselves, bringing in doctors, psychologists, sociologists, and lawyers to provide advice and information that were readily accessible to readers. Lesbians and gay men, too, became researchers of their own communities, observing differences between geographically distant groups of sexual minorities, using sociological methods to consider the place of the deviant outsider and then not only to advocate for more understanding of sexual and gender minorities but also to encourage such minorities to rethink their personal or political approaches (Aldrich, 2006/1958; Cory, 1951). As Stephanie Foote (2005) argues, such concentration on the production and circulation of media, as well as on how to read oneself into communities, marks the growth of the sense of sexuality as culture—in her example, lesbian print culture. It would be a mistake, in other words, to assume that a particular revolt marks the beginning of the formation of communities when economic shifts that allowed gay people to move to the cities (D'Emilio, 1983) and even the formation of smaller publics, reading, meeting, and corresponding with another were already formed through readership and production of queer print materials (Foote, 2005).

Nevertheless, placing the beginnings of the social movement for sexuality and gender identity rights in the political context of the Stonewall riot may underscore a definitive shift into the public and into a mass organization. Further, Stonewall, with its defiant butch lesbian throwing the first punch and its multiracial, multisexuality, multigender alliance, demonstrates the importance of understanding minority sexuality as diverse. While there were and continue to be splits in LGBTQ politics along lines of gender, race, and gender identity, at least always starting the narratives that ground sexual orientation and gender identity with attention to diversity reminds diverse LGBTQ people to continue to challenge their racism, sexism, and transphobic bias. Stonewall is not the only beginning but it is a beginning that should bring attention to these intersecting aspects of sexual and gender identity.

Making Stonewall the start of the gay liberation movement also centralizes the often unstable and linked struggles for rights for minority sexualities and genders. Patrons of the Stonewall Inn included gay men, lesbians, bisexuals, and transgender, transsexual, and transvestite people. As active as transgender people have been in struggles for gay rights, they have also been excluded by those in the gay rights movement seeking rights for only a limited, respectable-appearing segment of the LGBTQ community. Stonewall also stands as a reminder that even radical movements enact exclusions (Frye, 2002).

Uprisings such as the Stonewall riots underscore both the experience of harassment, exclusion, and the ability of people to resist. That resistance further points to the fact that communities were already organized and understood themselves to have developed the expectation of respect and legibility to one another as members. But by focusing on riots or uprisings as if the protest were the focal point and not either an outcome of longer struggle or the start of even more work, such histories diminish the lifetimes of effort that go into creating change. Participants in the Stonewall riots such as Sylvia Rivera, a

Latina transwoman and Marsha P. Johnson, an African American transwoman, also formed alliances with other political movements active at the time, including the Black Panthers and Young Lords, pushing them to recognize gender, gender identity, and sexuality-related issues. Organizing the Street Transvestite Action Revolutionaries, they developed service for transgender women in need of food, shelter, and community. Their contributions, including decades long work to have the rights of transgender people recognized, shows a commitment to changing laws and a commitment to ensuring that communities have the opportunity and means to thrive through their own efforts.

To be clear, movements and uprisings are also interlinked. Indebted to the Civil Rights Movement, the gay liberation movement often modeled itself after activism aimed at improving the lives of people of color. In part, this was so because some gay liberation activists were people of color and in part because the civil rights and Black power movements set the standard for activism during the 1960s. Activists within civil rights, Black feminism, women of color feminism, and Black power groups pushed the gay, women's, and lesbian movements to be aware of racism, and leaders in various movements urged their members to be critical of their dislike of gay people (Anzaldúa, 1990; Clarke, 1981, 1983; Smith, 1983). This was by no means a simple process or a utopian moment; movements were also energetically split on whether addressing minority sexuality and gender identity would delegitimize their claims or open them to ridicule. For instance, Betty Friedan, leader of the National Organization for Women, characterized lesbian involvement in the women's movement as a "lavender menace" (as cited in Brownmiller, 1970, p. 140). Civil rights leaders involved in the 1963 March on Washington had wanted Bayard Rustin removed as the lead organizer of the march when his homosexuality became known. Only through the intercession of A. Phillip Randolph was Rustin kept in charge (D'Emilio, 2003), though later he was excluded from prominent roles in the Civil Rights Movement. The same tendency to exclude or ignore LGBTQ members of dominant communities is also paralleled in minority communities.

LGBTQ communities are often structured by White dominance and are unwilling to see how Whiteness structures ideas about who is legitimately LGBTQ or who can easily access LGBTQ community resources and social spaces. This White dominance may be expressed through overt racism or implicitly assume what gayness means and thus be unwilling to recognize the sexual and gender identities that emerge within racial and ethnic communities. Exclusions within minority communities continue today through informal messages about the unacceptability or unrespectability of LGBTQ people of color (Duncan, 2005; Kumashiro, 2001, 2002, 2003) as well as through political debate in minority communities about HIV/AIDS (Cohen, 1999).

Even though there may not always be sustained attention to diversity within groups organizing for social justice, by focusing on moments and strands within movements that acknowledge their complicity in forms of bias, we can see that *multiculturally influenced politics*—a politics attentive to multiple forms of diversity—has been a part of almost every political movement. Indeed, historian Herbert Aptheker (1992) has asked why so many histories of social movements are framed only as interested in their own issues and represented as if they were made up of relatively homogeneously identified people. He asks us to consider how the expectation that people will work only on their own behalf has limited our contemporary ability to imagine diversely organized politics. Even at the height of what has come to be known as the heyday of identity politics, many groups were calling their own prejudices into question and making connections across struggles and identities. Black Panther founder Huey Newton (1973), for instance, argued that all movements needed to challenge their biases, including sexism and homophobia and learn to work together in common cause:

> Whatever your personal opinions and your insecurities about homosexuality and the various liberation movements among homosexuals and women (and I speak of the homosexuals and women as oppressed groups), we should try to unite with them in a revolutionary fashion. . . . I do not remember our ever constituting any value that said that a revolutionary must say offensive things towards homosexuals, or that a revolutionary should make sure that women do not speak out about their own particular kind of oppression. As a matter of fact, it is just the opposite: we say that we recognize the women's right to be free. We have not said much about the homosexual at all, but we must relate to the homosexual movement because it is a real thing. And I know through reading, and through my life experience and observations, that homosexuals are not given freedom and liberty by anyone in the society. They might be the most oppressed people in the society. (p. 143)

Other groups such as the Black feminist Combahee River Collective opposed ranking oppressions. They viewed oppressions as "interlocking," including race, gender, class, and sexuality as part of a critique of unequal social relations but also pointed out the pervasiveness of racism, even among White people who seemed to be politically aware (Combahee River Collective, 1982). By taking account of the intersections of categories of identity, it becomes clear that the identities of all people are multiple. By examining the critiques of the various rights and liberation movements, we can further understand that all communities are made up of diverse people, not all of whom are adequately served by the community norms or political groups that claim to represent them. Furthermore, forms of gender and sexual identity emerge from within different cultural, racial, and ethnic traditions and thus push us to understand the importance of place, context, and relation. Transnational immigration brings diverse understandings of sexual and gender identity into conversation with dominant versions, and racial and ethnic traditions provide particular forms of gender and sexual identities and activities that inform, challenge, and mingle with dominant forms (Manalansan, 2003).

In addition to these forms of diversity, the beginnings of gay liberation at the Stonewall Inn were also a combination of older and younger gender and sexual minority people, as well as heterosexual activists who joined by the second night of the riots. One account points out both the young age and disreputability of those who are now considered to have started the gay rights movement:

> They were street kids. They were very young runaways and castaways leaving their families, or thrown out, because they were gay. Many of them were homeless and lived precarious (and sometimes short) lives by hustling, petty thievery, drug dealing, and odd jobs. Others were weekend street kids, kids who led double lives; straight at home and at school, and gay on the weekends in Manhattan. They too sometimes hustled and dealt drugs. As one gay Village resident who knew them said, "They were rotten kids, but they were made rotten." (Blanchard, 2009)

From the start, then, the organized movement for gay liberation was more than something for people who might have been labeled gay—it involved youth rebellion and people whose lives couldn't be defined by respectability; it involved public expression of pleasure and perversity and people of all races and genders whose lives were more defined around street life than school life. But we can also see that as the movement organized, that complexity was removed by some seeking more respectability—early links with movements for racial justice and trans rights got shunted aside, sexism in the movement increased, and so on. The beginnings of movements for change can also date to the beginning of queer trans rebellion calling for more inclusive community institutions, for health care and support, and for the end to police harassment of transpeople. The 1966 Compton Cafeteria riots, where transvestite and transgender patrons, mostly sex workers, rebelled when harassed by police, reinforced both a sense of possibility and a link to other movements demanding rights but also wanting to develop self-sustaining community. Like Stonewall in some ways, the Compton riots were started by a diverse group, and gave an indication that gender identity and what we might now think of as queerness or genderqueer cannot be separated from thinking about gay liberation. Trans politics, like gay politics, also involves rethinking bodies, calling for changes in medical practices and technologies, critiquing social institutions of gender while working on the margins of economic relations, often in danger but sometimes blending into respectability and passing, though class and race complicate any claims about passing and normativity.

Any origin story of LGBTQ politics starts a narrative that creates different connections among struggles, and the history of political struggle inevitably winds together gender and sexuality. A different origin might be found with 19th-century marriage resisters, in which case we would centralize a critique of patriarchal gender relations as the start. Another origin of LGBTQ politics and community could start with women who passed as men, a beginning that would highlight the economic inequalities faced by women and also connect those to the gender-related economic struggles that were part of the Compton and Stonewall riots. Yet other beginnings of demands for sexual and gender rights start with movements for the rights of sex workers or the forced institutionalization of gender and sexuality nonconforming youth. We might start with the Harlem Renaissance and the broadening influence of arts and literature from the Black communities, not just trying out new ways of living but making ways of living and relating part of the spectacle of art and joy.

Each place we begin leads us to different narratives of how and where sexuality and gender function to create communities, and further, how creativity and innovation—or even just older, traditional understandings of sexual and gendered possibility—drive other formations. We can also push back to women's entrance into higher education and their ability to live without heterosexual marriage. We could make the same observation of men in military service, a kind of homosocial or gender segregated life that enabled them to create intimate ties with one another. The origins of movements for sexuality and gender–related rights might also start with formerly enslaved people demanding a continuation of complex family arrangements that couldn't be covered by marriage (Franke, 2004). Each time we resituate our opening, we draw in more strands of political critique and different communities. These are only the most slender start of what resituating movements for change can do to help rethink the relationship among diverse forms of identity.

Each time we trace a different sort of origin or open the subject differently, we may find that we have gotten further from what we now understand sexuality to be and mean. The simple point is that by tracing each of these origins, we get a different view of what sexuality means. The same complex conceptual, historical, and political work should be done with heterosexuality. Heterosexuality is itself a relatively new invention, and its origins are closely linked to how definitions of homosexuality, as we commonly understand it today, got started (Katz, 2007). The anxieties surrounding both formations as sexuality are not dissimilar. The term heterosexuality was coined by Karoly Kertbeny and was either an attempt to equalize same-gender and different-gender relationships, or was meant to indicate people who defined themselves by their gender orientation in a way that implied there was something wrong with that (Katz, 2007). In other words, heterosexuality had a tinge of problem to it; and because this was the mid-19th century and gender and sexual relations were already the stuff of social problems, anxieties continued to follow heterosexuality. By the time U.S. doctors are dealing with the problem of heterosexuality in 1892, it emerges as a problem defined by a desire for procreative and nonprocreative sex, with no particular gender object (Katz, 2007). Originally published in Latin in 1886 to prevent popular access, Kraft-Ebbing (1947), used the term heterosexual in a way that is closer to our current definition though his focus on heterosexual men who strangled their female partners does complicate that similarity. The point is that sexuality was studied as an extremely varied range of behaviors, clearly not all of which were normative. From the worries about seduction and free time, to the more 20th-century concerns with sex and dating exchanges ("treating" in the parlance of the time), heterosexuality, particularly youthful heterosexuality, has caused considerable consternation (Peiss, 1986). Just as you might hear people say they don't know what two men or two women could do with one another, the sex advice columns of the 1950s, 1960s, 1970s, and even today indicate that the definition for sexual acts—who can do what to whom when and so on—are all unsettled questions. We have all grown up being shaped by these histories even if we don't think about it explicitly, and even if we don't know the details of the histories.

SCHOOLS AND THE HISTORIES OF GENDER IDENTITY AND SEXUAL ORIENTATION

As I pointed out earlier, schools have long been concerned that teachers and students comport themselves respectably and that they conform to gender norms. Heteronormativity, the assumption that heterosexuality is the only sexual orientation, shapes all of our upbringings as much as does the anxiety that it isn't. In other words, careful attention to gender normativity, whether of students, teachers, or administrators, indicates a cultural fear that people will act in nonconforming ways or that critique of norms is possible, even barely kept in check. School architecture, policies, and institutional norms all structure an educational world in which heterosexuality is the only publicly sanctioned identity, but all those histories are haunted as well by the presence of single women learning in colleges and seeing new possibilities beyond traditional families, men in close quarters with one another sharing emotional and physical intimacies, and the open secrets of gay and lesbian teachers, whether among the first generation of women professors, teachers, or school administrators. Even before sexualities became codified by law, medicine, and psychology as distinct identities, people involved in education knew longer histories that connected learning with sexuality, whether from the classics or their own school experiences. Passion is not only about sexual desire; it also characterizes the energetic desire for more learning, for finding out new ideas, and helps bind together communities of inquiry. And the connections among youth, the pleasures of learning, and the ways in which teachers are role models for young people also challenge cultural and religious ideas about sexuality and schooling. Anita Bryant led a successful campaign in Dade County, Florida, taken up elsewhere in the United States during 1977 to repeal gay employment protections in general and to drive gay and lesbian teachers out of their jobs. Jackie Blount's *Fit to Teach* (2006) and Karen Graves' *And They Were Wonderful Teachers* (2009) both describe the history of teaching as a profession and how teaching developed as an occupation that was particularly tied to cultural anxieties over gender and same-sex desire. Blount details the long duration of teaching and administration as fields that regulated gender: requirements that young women teachers, for instance, be unmarried and that they dress and comport themselves in gender-conforming ways in order to model correct gender to their students. She notes that these concerns eventually developed into cultural anxieties about the "strange manner" (Blount, 2006, p. 60) in which spinster teachers were reproducing themselves by encouraging female students to become (heterosexually) unattached women and go into teaching and that female teachers were making boys effeminate. Graves (2009) details the purge of gay and lesbian teachers in Florida just after the Red Scare and the Lavender Scare, but before later anti-gay teacher activism in the 1970s. Her account stands as a reminder that the pressures for teachers to be heterosexual have taken shape in different political contexts but that much of the bias shaping those efforts have had marked similarities and used similar tactics of coercion. Education, then, has been a field determined to exclude gender and sexual minorities, but has also been populated with LGBTQ teachers for a long time.

Curricular inclusion of gay-related information has also had a contentious history. As newer legislation and curricula seek to limit how LGBTQ issues can be addressed in schools, remembering earlier links between sexual and gender minority issues and multiculturalism can help remind us of the stakes of such connections (Humm, 1994; Lee, Murphy, North, Ucelli, 2000). Controversy broke out in New York City in the early 1990s over the multicultural education teachers' guide *Children of the Rainbow* (New York City Board of Education, 1994). The guide included suggestions for lessons on the diversity of family structures—including gay and lesbian families. The goal was to help all students feel comfortable and valued in school. While the earlier outcry over the multicultural New York State social studies standards had mobilized social conservatives to work against inclusion of lessons on racial diversity, the controversy over the *Rainbow* curricula marked a switch in tactics with social conservatives advocating for the inclusion of so-called legitimate minorities but not minority sexual orientation or families (Mayo, 2004a). *Children of the Rainbow* was not the first time sexual orientation was recognized in New York City's educational policy. The New York City Board of Education had included sexual orientation as a protected class since 1985 (New York City Board of

Education), but *Children of the Rainbow* was the first concerted effort to bring sexual minority issues into the multicultural curriculum.

A 2011 law in California requires that school districts adopt textbooks on U.S. history that include lessons on the contributions of LGBTQ people. As schools continue to widen the range of inclusiveness in curricula, laws like these may encourage textbook makers as well as educational professionals to widen their understanding of diversity. While knowing more about the history of sexual orientation, gender identity, and political movements organized around them is one way to open these questions and to understand that sex, sexuality, and gender are all issues deserving of serious scholarship and education, clearly there are more barriers to educating about LGBTQ issues than one might face in other subjects.

Narrating origins of LGBTQ communities through uprisings, on the one hand, and through persistent communities, on the other hand, underscores the complexities of living under normative systems with difficulty, but also with making meaning and community in the context of that struggle. By focusing on the moments of conflict and the particular people injured by bias, do we imply that those groups and identities have meaning only because of their clash with dominant culture? Is the story of oppression and bias the only way schools are willing to even begin to address sexual and gender minorities? By focusing only on minority sexualities and their experience of bias, schools neglect to examine the relationship between the dominant sexuality's claim to normalcy and the resultant heterosexism and heteronormativity of the curricula, institutional organization, and school policies. By thinking of heterosexism and homophobia as evident only in spectacles of bias—such as homophobic injury, assault, or murder—the everyday forms of heterosexism go unremarked, as does the everyday presence of people who do not conform to gender and sexual norms. If teachers are unwilling to acknowledge and educate about the positive aspects of sexuality, they also neglect the relationship between sexuality and identity; miss the place of sexuality in initiating and sustaining personal, cultural, and community relationships; and reinforce the unacceptability of educating about sexuality and pleasure. By not focusing on these histories in relationship to other struggles for equality, lessons also miss the conversations and changes that happened as a result of diverse movements talking to one another.

CHAPTER 2

Thinking Through Biases and Assumptions About LGBTQ People

Drawing on theories discussing gender as a process, homophobia, and intersectionality, this chapter examines the pervasiveness of heteronormativity and the varieties of queerness to help readers understand where bias comes from, as well as be attuned to differences in the experiences of gender nonconforming and/or sexual minority students. Looking at the roots of homophobia in bias against nonconforming genders will help link homophobia to transphobia and sexism as well. Examining sexuality as racialized and gendered, in turn, will illuminate differences in experiences of sexual minority students across diverse identities and provide a fuller understanding of how race structures sexuality. This chapter will help readers understand the theories of gender, sexuality, and race that have influenced writing and research on LGBTQ students as well as helped structure current LGBTQ and ally political projects in schools.

GENDER AS PROCESS

In her book *Gender Play: Girls and Boys at School*, Barrie Thorne (1993) researches how and why gender comes to have salience in young people's school experiences. Practices like having elementary students line up by gender or organizing teams of boys against girls, she argues, highlights the importance of gender differences to young students at a time when they are also working through different ways of being gendered themselves. Concerned that the institutional culture of schools not only creates rigid ideas about gender but also pits one gender against the other, she suggests that adults in schools consider more carefully the messages about gender that even simple practices, like making gender-based small groups or encouraging gender-segregated play, convey to young people. Thorne shows too that gender salience ebbs and flows, and that students understand and rework the gender binary messages they receive. Even as her work pushes us to think beyond simple questions about what gender is and instead look at how and why gender differences emerge in particular situations, her work shows that gender and negotiations over its meaning continue to highlight cultural desires about normalcy, conformity, complementarity between genders, and so on.

Heterosexism and *heteronormativity*, the beliefs and social practices that maintain the dominance of heterosexuality over other forms of sexuality, rely on a stable conception of binary genders. Men have to act in accordance with norms regulating masculinity and women need to be feminine not only in order for their genders to be legible in expected ways but also to justify the "opposites attract" version of heterosexuality. Gender and sexuality, then, sort out who is "normal," and the categories provide norms that interact with one another. People of all sexualities and genders experience these social pressures to conform, whether they actively try to conform or they are nonconformist or they don't even know they are trying to conform. In other words, gender and sexuality are categories by which life in schools and elsewhere is organized, and understanding those norms frames everyone's experience even if they are involved in critiquing those norms. Gender nonconformity and sexual minority status may be linked by school peers inaccurately, exacerbating the harassment transgender youth face (D'Augelli, Grossman, & Starks, 2006). Moreover, LGBTQ students themselves may express their identities through both gender and sexuality nonconformity.

Understanding the interplay of normative identities, intersections of identity categories, and creative reworkings of norms and categories can help provide better strategies for members of school communities to consider their own practices more carefully and to challenge how normativity and homophobia create barriers to education for all students. One way to think about the roots of homophobia is to think about how gender normativity—what counts as a "normal" male or female—gets taught and learned. How do genders become understood as having particular qualities, actions, appearances, and so on? How do gender identity and sexual orientation, stabilized as normative, then become the foundation for the normative and normal communities and personal relationships? To understand these processes within schools, Thorne (1993) looks at not only adult expectations and definitions, but also the general tendency of institutions, especially educational institutions, to sort and label its members. Her work pushes us to see as well that countermoves follow each of these institutional moves: The elementary school students whose classroom work and playground activities she observes in her study play with gender as a *border category*, that is, a category whose meanings are understood but also open to challenge.

Thorne's (1993) point is that such negotiations of gender are part of all students' experience. Research on sexual harassment points to ways that girls especially feel pressure to conform to gendered norms or feel the hostility of gender dynamics especially keenly (AAUW, 2001). Transgender students, too, understand how difficult it is to negotiate the dynamics of gender difference and conformity, having to strategize their own gender identity in the context of social expectations unused to their innovative approaches to enacting gender or refusing their birth gender. In some situations, their peers understand how the issues raised by transgender students can help all students rethink gender norms and expression, but very often transgender students face exclusion and bias in schools. Transgender students themselves may also feel pressured to conform to the gender binary, hiding their birth gender or deciding to be as gender normative in their chosen gender as possible so as not to raise any suspicions (Bochenek & Brown, 2001; Ehrensaft, 2013).

Youth, of course, are already engaged in these reworkings of social norms whether in school or out. In her discussion of the resistances of queer street youth, Cindy Cruz (2011) demonstrates youth of color who are resistant in the face of institutional disrespect. Her work shows that queer and transyouth have well-honed practices of talking back and of providing support to one another in difficult situations. For instance, when one young transwoman is being treated brusquely by EMTs, her friend changes the meaning of the scene by declaring the ambulance sirens to be in her honor: "Look at that. You such a diva that they had to announce with sirens that you weren't feeling good" (p. 552). The complexity of gender and sexuality are interwoven, as well, with messages, definitions, and reworkings of the meanings of other categories of identity like race, ethnicity, social class, disability, and religion, among others. In her discussion of an after-school meeting space for young queers of color, Mollie Blackburn (2005) describes another form of talking back: speaking in slang both to assert public identity and to maintain a degree of privacy. These moments of resistance, like Thorne's discussion of younger students' gender play, stand as reminders that young people of color create their own support systems in the midst of contexts that are otherwise challenging. But they are also reminders that young people and young adults, as in Cruz's research, may find adult responses inadequate and even damaging.

Thorne's work, like other approaches to gender that focus on the process of social construction, pushes us to ask how and why gender comes to have salience and stability in some contexts and how it comes to be in play in others. For Mindy Blaise (2005), early childhood educators need to understand the pressures young people are facing and be proactive in raising the possibilities for gender play and gender critique. When teachers help students look more explicitly at the processes and instabilities that define gendered interactions, they can begin to see patterns of gendered exclusions more clearly themselves. Students themselves also initiate these discussions and show that they can have a good sense of why some contexts overstabilize complex meanings—and potentially create hostilities against those whose behavior or identity does not conform to normative expectations (Boldt, 1996). While Thorne (1993) argues that young people's play opens the possibilities of ambiguities in meanings of gender and sexuality, giving space for young girls to be athletic or boys to sit at the "girls'" table or play in the "girls'" area of the playground, she also shows that such occasions of playful attempts to cross the gender divide can be met with hostility and that teasing can cross over the line of play and into harassment.

Despite pressures to conform to normative gender, gender remains in play. While this sense of play may open possibilities, play with gender or play with sexuality also raises anxieties and bias against transgender and gender nonconforming youth. Such bias and harassment affects gender nonconforming, transgender, or cisgender youth at a higher rate than gender conforming youth and may come from peers or school personnel (Grossman & D'Augelli, 2006). By suggesting to adults that there are more possible identities for students to inhabit than adults might consider normal or even possible, such play may indicate not only adult insufficiency of understanding but also perhaps adult lack of control of young people's identities. Unexpected differences in identity or behavior may seem to break rules, even rules that adults think didn't need to be articulated like those indicating that boys and girls, or young men and young women, dress in particularly gendered ways. Recently a 14-year-old Florida student, who preferred not to share his sexual identity, was punished for wearing makeup to school (Sieczkowski, 2013). The principal claimed the student was in violation of the dress code, but the dress code had no reference to make up (Sieczkowski, 2013). Other similar situations, including a young women wearing a suit (Esseks, 2010), a transgender student wanting to wear a dress (ACLU, 2013a), or simply cisgendered heterosexual students dressing in nonconforming ways have also led to principals requiring them to change clothes or remove makeup (Lui, 2011; Rasmus, 2013). Perhaps young people who defy expectations, too, raise larger issues of how much of what is normal needs to be explicitly taught and how much diversity ought to be allowed. Schools may fall back on insisting on normatively gendered behavior and in the process reinforce gender divisions and restrictions.

Gender restrictions, of course, affect everyone in schools. As young women continue to gain more access to athletic activities and educational and career advancement, older ideas about male–female relationships have changed; for instance, the necessity for feminine submissiveness to male power has significantly waned. Dress codes that prohibited women from wearing anything but skirts and dresses now generally seem old-fashioned. Increased attention to gender equity in education, through Title IX and other programs to get more young women interested in math and science, have had significant effects on the gender ratio in such fields in undergraduate education. Still, gender norms continue to function, putting a larger burden on heterosexually active young women to protect themselves from unwanted pregnancy and blaming them for their inability to control male sexual urges.

In addition, since many policies intent on helping address sexism have replicated a binary gender divide, transyouth and other gender nonconforming youth may face difficulties that go beyond policies intent on protecting women from bias. Moreover, transgender and cisgender women both face institutionalized sexism, though not in the same ways at all times.

Gender bias is also not only a problem for women. Young men who understand cultural messages about masculinity as encouraging their demonstration of superiority show their power through aggressive taunting. Whether because of pressure to conform to this problematic notion of male power or out of concern that they will be thought to be weak or gay if they don't harass, young men are the group most likely to harass LGBTQ youth and young cisgendered women as well. Even though we live in a time where gender norms continue to stretch, especially for women, schools are still institutions where gender sorting occurs, whether it is in the classroom or in community settings that debate policy and curricula. Sex education continues to be a relatively conservative part of schools, leading with abstinence-until-marriage messages that not only exclude most LGBTQ students, but also leave girls at disproportionate risk for unwanted pregnancy (not because—obviously—only girls can get pregnant, but because so few young men are taught to act as responsibly as young women or are not held responsible for the children that result).

SEXUALITY, NORMALCY, AND INTERSECTING DIFFERENCES

Like gender, sexuality, too, is an unstable and complex issue. While the purpose of this book is to show how LGBTQ issues can be addressed more educatively and productively in public schools, it is important to understand that challenging sexual and gender normativity can help people of all sexualities and genders. People may be able to easily say what would count as "normal," but they also know that conformity is difficult, if not impossible. Does sexuality involve only particular acts and particular genders in particular relationship to one another? How are sexual identities also defined by intense relationships, desires that may not be acted upon? How are attractions defined through ideas about gender, race, and class? In other words, as we think about making schools safer for sexual minorities, how do we even begin to address important issues, for instance, whether racial harassment is part of homophobia? Can we also think about how homophobic taunts are meant to keep all students maintaining a very narrow notion of what is appropriate to their gender? Thinking about how homophobia and anti-gay sentiment is used to keep all students in line can also help us see how assumptions about gender identity and sexuality overlap into bias against racial and ethnic minority students as well.

Some people, including school professionals, root their beliefs about gender norms or the inappropriateness of homosexuality in their cultural background or religious tradition. Cultural beliefs and religious texts are often interpreted to mean that LGBTQ people are aberrant, sinful, or at the very least unacceptable. Pushing beyond what seem to be determinative statements from a given culture or faith tradition often reveals a much more complex picture of the culture in which same-sex affection and partnership have long played an important role or in which various gender expressions have found support in a tradition. It may, of course, be difficult for adherents of particular religious traditions to embrace the same interpretations of the intensity of same-sex love and commitment within their texts that LGBTQ people of faith do or to even begin to grapple with the possibility that positive representations coexist with prohibitions against similar activities.

Further complicating the issue of sexual orientation and gender identity may be the sense that such forms of diversity and difference come from somewhere else, not from within a particular cultural tradition but imposed from outside. For instance, current dominant forms of homophobia may be directed at people who appear to be simply gay but are, in fact, living traditional, indigenous identities. Two-spirit people, that is, people who embody American Indian traditional practices that defy contemporary definitions of gender and sexuality, often find themselves harassed by those ignorant of the place of third genders and sexualities in indigenous cultures (Wilson, 1996). A commonplace assumption about homosexuality, not unrelated to the former example, is that all gay people are White, partially related to the White dominance in many gay communities and partially to the inability to see diversity as more than one aspect of identity at a time. Too often discussions of diversity seem to assume that all people have one identity, not that they might live complex lives in which their multiple differences intersect and affect one another.

When we begin to complicate what sexuality means in relation to race, class, gender, disability, region, and religion, it quickly becomes clear that we need to be thinking not only about multiple versions and variations of sexual identity but also about how different communities and contexts shape the life possibilities and definitions of sexual and gender identity of LGBTQ, queer, and gender minority people (Bello, Flynn, Palmer, Rodriguez, & Vente, 2004; Blackburn, 2004, 2005; Irvine, 1994; E. P. Johnson & Henderson, 2005; Kumashiro, 2004; Leck, 2000; McCready, 2010; Ross, 2005; Sears, 1995; Sonnie, 2000; Wilson, 1996). Minority sexualities and gender identities—like other differences within communities—are themselves reminders that not all in a given culture, race, ethnicity, or other seemingly similar coherent group are the same; there are differences within communities and subcultures structured around sexual orientation and gender identity. This may seem an obvious point, but dissent by members of communities from the sexual and/or gender norms of that community can result in a feeling that community norms have been disrupted and perhaps even a sense that the nonconformist person is a traitor to community cohesion.

Education against homophobia and about sexual minority issues needs to grapple with the cultural and traditional objections to sexual minority people and communities. Without addressing the deep cultural, political, and historical obstacles to educating LGBTQ people and educating about them, progress toward multicultural education and justice will be only halfhearted at best. While some religious traditions may be the root of some cultural disapproval of homosexuality, most religious traditions do not require their adherents to demand doctrinal discipline from those outside their faith tradition. Given the pervasiveness of homophobia even among people who do not ground their discomfort in religious traditions, it is clear that other anxieties also motivate discomfort about minority sexualities and gender identities. Many religious denominations are very supportive of sexual and gender minorities. Consequently, the tendency to blame religion for homophobia is an oversimplification. Denominations supportive of sexual and gender minorities include the Metropolitan Community Church, Reform Judaism, United Church of Christ, Society of Friends (Quakers), and Unitarianism, as well as segments of the Episcopal and Lutheran churches. Individual congregations of many faiths are also supportive of sexual and gender minorities.

As education against homophobia proceeds, it is necessary to find ways both to support people who experience homophobia and also to ask difficult questions about the cultural, religious, and contemporary roots of or alibis for homophobia. Acknowledging the existence of multiple cultural, local, and global forms of same-sex affection and gender variety may be one starting point. Examining the variety of expressions of tolerance and value of minority identities within minority and majority cultures may give insights into the differences that make up even seemingly coherent and unified cultures and subcultures. These issues should be familiar to anyone grappling with how to study and educate about any form of identity. But there are particular features to sex and gender identity that make addressing it challenging.

How much of homophobia is a reflection of cultural attitudes about sex in general and how particular objections to teaching about LGBTQ issues and sexuality are related to the young age of students (Silin, 1995)? How much of homophobia is bias against gender nonconforming behavior? Does homophobia reflect a cultural disparagement of femininity, or as some would put it, is homophobia a weapon of sexism (Pharr, 1997)? We can think here of the use of "girls" to insult young men and what that says about the pervasiveness of sexism. Does homophobia indicate anxiety about the fragility of the heterosexual norm? When even slight gender nonconforming behavior or friendship with someone of the same sex can begin rumors and harassment or when people feel compelled to assert their heterosexuality should doubt arise, we can see the process of normalization working on everyone. The ease with which such anxieties surface despite a climate of heterosexism that generally does not allow discussion of queer possibility indicates the haunting presence of queerness even in the midst of what is generally the unquestioned norm of heterosexuality.

In addition, homophobia has diverse roots, so being more aware of the different biases and anxieties behind its expressions can be key to challenging it and to challenging transphobia and other forms of exclusion as well. Even in the midst of thinking about bias and ensuring a fully educational response, there is a danger in letting homophobia define how and why lessons on sexual minorities are included in school. Institutional and legal restrictions have shaped the lives of sexual minority people, yet it would be a vast oversimplification to say that is the only reality of their lives. Sexuality, as discussed in the previous chapter, has a long and varied history—indeed histories of identities and subjectivities may bear little resemblance to the categories by which we currently define sexual identity. As much as those communities and identity formations were related to restrictions on their ability to live, they nonetheless formed cultures, associations, and—like other minorities living in a cultural context shaped by bias—reshaped their worlds. Tactically, it may be possible to convince people who do not initially want to include sexual minority issues in schooling that to do so would help address the risks that LGBTQ students face. However, we also need to be careful not to frame LGBTQ issues as only risk or deficit ones. When essays, such as this one, discussing the intersecting forms of bias related to homophobia and transphobia defensively cite statistics on harassment or provide a panel of LGBTQ people to describe their difficulties with homophobia, they miss the opportunity to examine the positive aspects of LGBTQ communities and cultures and the abilities of sexual minority people to live lives beyond institutional constraints.

LGBTQ youth of color report harassment that intersects their identities as LGBTQ and raced; and they report higher rates of homophobic harassment than they do racial harassment—but if we understand their identities as intersectional, that is, defined by race and sexuality, how do we even tease apart their negative experiences in schools? We might all know what sexual norms are, know as well that people don't conform to them and know further that we're not completely certain with all of these complications, what sex or sexual orientation is.

If we look at how sexual norms function to create and stabilize the meaning of gender, we get a better idea of the links between sex and power. In a classic article exploring the relationship between sexist cultural and political institutions and the way that heterosexuality becomes "compulsory" for women, feminist theorist and poet Adrienne Rich (1980) details how the assumption of heterosexuality is an active process of ensuring that women are dependent on men and that particular forms of gender identity that reinforce this heterosexual relationship are fostered in institutions like schools. Her conclusion is that all women have been actively kept from understanding and experiencing their sexuality because of gender and sexual norms. R. W. Connell (1987) and M. Kimmel (2010) each discuss similar processes of instilling normatively gendered behavior among young boys in order to educate them into normative sexuality that is defined through male dominance. Deborah Tolman (2006), in her research on adolescent girls, revisits Adrienne Rich's notion of compulsory heterosexuality to show how normative heterosexuality relies on hegemonic and interlocked definitions of masculinity and femininity. Tolman suggests that studying "gender complementarity," that is, how the hegemonic forms of each gendered identity encourage particular sorts of activities—for example, boys in groups boasting that they can get girls, and girls using femininity to hold them at bay—will provide us with a better picture of how gender functions in a social context defined by male power (p. 80). But she also cautions that such male power is not available to all men and so studying the way norms function can also help us understand how race, class, and sexuality position men outside of normative and hegemonic masculinity. Her work also has implications for thinking about how the normative gender binary restricts other possibilities of gender, including transgender identities.

Cathy Cohen's (1997) work on race and queer sexuality similarly analyzes how heteronormativity is raced and how racialization is also a process that positions non-White sexuality as non-normative. Using the example of slavery, she shows that people of African descent were unable to legally marry one another and that legacy coupled with laws against racial intermarriage marked out only Whiteness as a normative sexual category. Later pathologization of the Black family, the supposed recklessness of Black masculinity, or the dangers of Black welfare mothers continues, she argues, the process of defining normative sexuality not only by sexual orientation but by race, class, and gender as well. Schools, too, are prime sites for such contests over the meaning of race and sexuality. In his analysis of the intersections of race and sexual orientation in public schools, Lance McCready (2010) argues that schools need to be attentive to ensuring they address both racism and homophobia. His analysis of an in-school program for LGBTQ youth shows that LGBTQ youth of color are not able to access such a program because the overwhelmingly Whiteness and uninterrogated racism of white LGBTQ youth have yet to be adequately challenged.

TRANSPHOBIA IN SCHOOLS

Like the issues addressed in the previous section, the intersections between gender and gender identity have yet to be adequately addressed in schools. As Genny Beemyn (2013) points out, however, transgender issues are getting more attention, and increasingly the parents of transgender youth are acting as advocates for change:

> As trangender people achieve greater visibility in society and popular culture, more and more parents are becoming open to the possibility that their children might be transgender or gender nonconforming and seeking to understand their children's needs, rather than forcing them to deny who they are. As a result, we are witnessing the first generation of trans kids who can actually be trans kids. (pp. 159–160)

Whether parents are supportive or not—earlier studies have found them not to be (D'Augelli, Grossman, & Starks, 2006)—schools can respond thoughtfully. Even if school leaders, teachers, and counselors do not immediately fully understand how to educate transgender students, taking the time to explore access to restrooms, name and pronoun choice, and making sure that the entire school community responds with respect can ensure equitable educational access (Slesaransky-Poe, Ruzzi, Dimedio, & Stanley, 2013). Schools can indicate to parents a willingness to work together and even indicate the need for more study without being disrespectful. As one school guidance counselor put it, "I knew we were not ready yet, but I saw no reason why we couldn't be, and I knew we had a responsibility to become the right school for Martin" (Slesaransky-Poe et al., 2013, p. 31). Further, learning with parents to ask key questions and being willing to understand how to rethink gender and gender identity norms simultaneously means that critical awareness of such issues will impact more than the transgender students in the school.

Transgender students and their parents may choose to use hormone blockers to allow young people more time to think carefully and decide on their chosen gender without having to go through hormonal changes and the development of secondary sexual characteristics that may make such choices more challenging (Ehrensaft, 2013). Students may decide that they prefer "going stealth" at school rather than having their decision become public (Ehrensaft, 2013, p. 10). While being out and public may work for some students and may help an entire school community prepare for a student's or faculty member's transition, the choice to remain private also needs to be respected with transgender students as with sexual minority students. Transgender students may also be concerned that they will be misrecognized as the gender they were formerly known as or that they will be misrecognized as transgender when they instead want to be known by their chosen gender. For some young people, a normative binary gender does not adequately express their gender complexity, but for others, being recognized only as the gender they are is crucial.

Gender complexity is as difficult to negotiate for researchers as it may be for school professionals—students are increasingly innovative in the new formations of gender and self-identifications they use. As Greytak, Kosciw, and Boesen (2013) found, such complications meant removing students from their study's results because their identification on forms confounded the researchers' expectations for categories. They explain:

> Participants were also excluded from the current study if they did not provide information about their gender identity or if they could not be categorized as either cisgender or as transgender (i.e., participants who, in response to the gender identity item, wrote in that they were another gender—for example, genderqueer or pangender—and also did not select a transgender response option; see the Measures section for information on how gender identity was categorized). (p. 49)

Other students surveyed used terms available but combined them in ways it sounds like researchers weren't expecting:

> When asked about their gender identity, some youth selected both male and transgender or selected both female and transgender (but not male-to-female or female-to-male). These youth were categorized as "transgender and female" and "transgender and male." Other youth in our sample identified as both male and female or both male-to-female and female-to-male and were categorized as "multigender" for the purposes of this study. (Greytak, Kosciw, & Boesen, 2013, p. 51)

Whatever the complications of student identifications and self-understandings, Greytak, Kosciw, and Boesen (2013) found that transgender students experienced more benefits associated with schools having nondiscrimination policies, anti-bullying policies, and GSAs.

Different kinds of complications may also arise from students, cisgender or not, trying to sort out gender normative identity and behavior from gender nonconforming identities and behaviors. Boldt (1996) found elementary students willing to recognize cross-gender identifications but also noted that some students objected to their classmates' willingness to identify students in their preferred gender. She suggests that both this uncertainty indicates not only a complex understanding of gender but also a recognition that children are looking to adults for some signal about gender correctness, a point that also reinforces Thorne's (1993) analysis of the relationship between gender differences being made more apparent in a context where an adult is present.

In their study, C. L. Ryan, Patraw, and Bednar (2013) found elementary students brought up complications to and refusals of gender norms on their own. Elementary students also explained nonconforming gender in peers, showing that they were not only already in the company of students whose gender identity exceeded binaries, but that they could also begin to reflect on such experiences in class. C. L. Ryan et al. (2013) found that their vocabularies for such experiences were not completely accurate, but the students were not ignorant of the general issues around gender nonconformity and the limitations of gender norms. The teacher and coauthor with whom C. L. Ryan et al. researched added her own concerns that students understand exclusions based on gender identity as connected to other forms of school-based bias and bullying. Like Rands's (2013) use of mathematics education to encourage students to study the degree to which peers intervene in bias, C. L. Ryan et al. (2013) show a classroom structured around understanding the intersections of oppression and discrimination and, further, knowing how to plan to step in to support someone being bullied. Each of these lessons draws all students into a consideration of the limitations of gender norms—something they are already engaged in themselves—and also helps them think educatively and constructively about intervening in situations where gender norms are being used to limit classmates' ability to express their own gender. Gender itself is placed in relation to other categories of exclusion, and so the particularity of gender identity bias or transphobia are specifically attended to while other issues are entwined as well.

As students are engaging with the issues of gender, they inevitably raise questions about sexism, about what expectations for gender mean, and why we become so attached not only to normative gender but also relatedly to normative sexuality. Kate Bornstein (1994) complicates gender identity by describing her own experience of the disconnection between her assigned gender and her gender identity not as a positive connection with womanhood but a negation of boyhood:

> I've no idea what a "woman" feels like. I never did feel like a girl or a woman; rather it was my unshakable conviction that I was not a boy or a man. It was the absence of a feeling, rather than its presence, that convinced me to change my gender. . . . Gender identity answers another question: "to which gender (class) do I want to belong?" Being and belonging are closely related concepts when it comes to gender. I felt I was a woman (being), and more importantly I felt I belonged with other women. (p. 24)

This narrative may trouble the idea that transgender people only choose their gender for one reason or that inevitably they must subscribe to the feeling of being trapped in the wrong body, rather than also literally embodying a critique of the gender they were born into. Bornstein (1994) complicates, too, what belonging to a gender means in a sexist society in her analysis of how passing is discussed in transsexual and transvestite meetings she attended:

> A lot of emphasis was given to manners: who stands up to shake hands? Who exits an elevator first, who opens doors? Who lights cigarettes? These are all cues I had to learn in order to pass as a woman in this culture. It wasn't 'til I began to read feminist literature that I began to question these cues or see them as oppressive. (p. 29)

Like the students in Greytak et al.'s study (2013), then, Bornstein (1994) suggests a critical reading of gender can be coextensive with a change in embodied gender. In other words, transgender identity does not need to mean conforming to the other gender norm. Just as students created alliances across differences of gender identity and sexual orientations, Bornstein points to the need for a greater understanding of relationality in identity and common struggles with sexism, racism, and other forms of bias. Connecting transgender activism more firmly into feminism can also help highlight areas of overlap between gender-related struggles, challenge ideas about stable gender binaries, and open possibilities for new kinds of gender identities (Enke, 2012).

QUEER RELATIONALITIES

As we think about what queer theory can do to complicate our commonplace understandings of gender, especially in regard to how schools try to reproduce gender norms, we need to think critically about the damaging aspects of such fidelity to the stability of gender identity and sexual identity. We need to think critically as well about the diversities of those identities whether complicated by the varieties of meanings of sex and gender as they intersect with other forms of identity and community, or whether they are complex within a given person's life and experience. Queer theory not only complicates what we mean by sexuality and gender, it expands whom we're talking about when we're talking about queer. If we all live under cultural norms that oversimplify gender and sexuality in problematic ways that have no purpose other than the reproduction of norms, then people of all sexualities have much to gain by countering entrenched homophobia and transphobia, not only because excluding students, faculty, staff, and community members is unethical but also because such norms are limiting to everyone. Queer theory asks us to think critically about words that are often excluded from curricula: pleasure, perversity, possibility.

If all sexualities and genders do share a critical relationship to key categories of identity, then thinking about identity relationally may be one way to indicate this shared fate and shared possibility for change. Especially given the increasing attention to family members and friends of LGBTQ people, thinking about identities as "identifying with and identifying as" gives us new ways of situating LGBTQ-seeming issues in a broader social field. Emphasizing relationality between genders and sexualities does not indicate that LGBTQ issues on their own aren't worthy of notice. Kids of gay parents experience homophobia, many kids are exposed to homophobic taunts, and kids learn in contexts where LGBTQ information is largely missing from the curriculum. As a result, all students learn that this exclusion is meaningful to who they should become. This point simply returns us to Eve Sedgwick's (1990) conception of universalizing discussions of gayness, that is, looking at how homophobia and same-sex desires suffuse almost all social interaction. We might follow a similar sort of intellectual trajectory in the research from either the early homophile movement or gay liberation or lesbian feminism to find other understandings of how much homosexuality/fear of homosexuality/fear of being considered a homosexual/fear of same-sex desire (one's own or someone else's) has created the social identity of the purportedly straight as much as it has allowed the proliferation of every other sort of sexuality.

The simple point here is that heteronormativity is as fractured and riddled with cultural anxieties as any other dominant social formation. Perversion of the norm is more widespread than might be apparent if only focusing on LGBTQ people. Norms, in other words, are so impossible to follow that everyone invariably transgresses them. The heteronormative school practices and educational research are not only functional as limits to what can be thought about sexuality, they are also indications of a certain degree of ignorance, if they really are meant to describe what goes on in sexual identity, activity, and fantasy, let alone community and representation. That various state legislators are interested in passing laws to prevent teachers from saying the word *gay* or addressing questions students might have about sexual orientation or answering students' questions about sexuality in gender indicate persistent concerns about maintaining heteronormativity. Such attempts to legally limit learning about sexual orientation and sexuality also indicate an understanding that young people will ask such questions and that teachers could potentially help them think more fully about those issues than schools currently allow. Research on bullying and bias shows just how ubiquitous and damaging heteronormativity and gender normativity are, but bias and harassment are processes that are also ineffective: not everyone bullies, not everyone conforms. Young people play through and around categories, assert themselves against institutional power, and simply find people with whom to build pleasurable and supportive networks. But on the issue of cruelty, listening to youth of any variety of sexualities including heterosexual tell me that they can't take consent forms home because their parents would be angry leads me to think that one of the reasons it would be hard to study how straight parents experience schools when their kids are gay is that many of them don't know their kids aren't straight, or if their kids do identify as heterosexual, parents may not know that they also identify with the struggles of their LGBTQ peers against gender and sexual normativity. So even as heteronormativity does not always operate to completely limit consideration of gender or sexual non-normativity, sexual and gender norms operate and circulate well enough to keep the LGBTQ youth worried that they will be kicked out of their houses or disrespected at school. They do resist, but they are also already in institutions that are structured by well-meaning teachers staging debates on same-sex marriage or addressing sexuality as abstinence-based lessons with more silence than content in contexts where same-gender partners attending prom still create controversy. This all only adds to how cruel the school setting can be, with its already palpable rumble of heteronormative institutional structure. But clearly in all of this, the queer, questioning, and ally kids learn a lot and they have much to teach as well.

This points to what we can learn from the vernacular forms of youth sexuality and gender questioning and curiosity and a range of other formations that show the contextual possibility and complexity of gender identity. There are youth who are bigendered in the sense that in particular settings or affective states they will be gendered in distinctly different ways and youth whose racial or ethnic identity may be their primary identification and site of solidarity, showing how diversities challenge what are sometimes taken to be key features of life, like coming out and/or hiding in plain sight. There are heterosexual girls in Gay-Straight Alliances—which seems to indicate that such groups are not yet attracting the students who need them (Perrotti & Westheimer, 2001)—who then turn out to have interesting ideas about their own definitions of heterosexuality and their queer experiences, reminding us that young people are often more complex than they might initially present themselves (Mayo, 2007). Young men who reinterpret their experiences of homophobic hostility as an indication of interest in finding out more about same-sex attraction (McCready, 2010) and young people who rework gender for themselves—and to show what can be done—are engaging in acts of resistance but also acting as educators themselves. They show not only interest and desire to learn but a clear sense of what criticality might bring to the projects of sexuality and gender, resituating the terms more fully back into possibilities and back into relation with other categories of personal, social, and historical meaning.

CHAPTER 3

Specific School-Related Challenges Facing LGBTQ Students

Experiences of harassment, assault, or simply not seeing any representation of LGBTQ lives in the curricula all contribute to negative school-based experiences. This chapter details recent studies and theoretical work on the hostile climate in schools, examines gaps in curricula, and discusses family-related issues that also challenge LGBTQ students or students with LGBTQ parents. These may include a lack of role models in schools, discomfort with parental involvement or, especially in the case of children with LGBTQ parents, difficult relations between school and family (Kosciw & Diaz, 2008). In keeping with our focus on the diversity of LGBTQ experiences, this chapter continues an analysis of the intersections of racial, gendered, and gender identity–related violence, harassment, and alienation that students in public school and family settings experience. The particular implications for schools' intervention in bias and provision of spaces for organizing LGBTQ students and allies to learn from one another are discussed as necessary for ensuring the educational success of LGBTQ students.

Schools, like the rest of the social world, are structured by heterosexism—the assumption that everyone is and should be heterosexual (that such an assumption should have to be stated or even reinforced by policies indicates everyone might not be heterosexual but they should be). Curricula, texts, school policies, and even mundane examples, such as illustrations of magnets showing males attracted to females but repulsed by one another, are most often constructed to reflect that heterosexuality is not only the norm but also the only possible option for students (Friend, 1995). Heterosexism is also reinforced by homophobia, overt expressions of dislike, harassment, and even assault of sexual minority people, a practice that members of the school community often ignore or dismiss as typical behavior based on the heterosexist assumption that either there are no LGBTQ people present in school communities, or, if there are, those LGBTQ people ought to learn to expect a hostile environment. While homophobia may possibly be—at least in some places—less socially acceptable today than it was previously, it is nonetheless the case that schools are not very supportive places for most LGBTQ, questioning, intersex, and ally students. The pressure to conform to rigid ideas about proper gender and sexuality is also damaging to heterosexual and gender conforming students as well. Many students of all sexual orientations have experienced anti-gay or gender identity–related harassment so teaching all students to be respectful of gender and sexuality diversity helps everyone.

Members of school communities may believe that sexuality is not an appropriate topic for young people. However, there are significant numbers of LGBTQ and ally students in schools, as well as significant numbers of sexually aware heterosexual students. Ignoring the issue of sexuality means neglecting to provide LGBTQ students with representations of themselves that enable them to understand themselves, and to provide examples of ways to counter bias and work toward respect for those who may not initially be willing to respect LGBTQ students. Many LGBTQ students report hearing insulting words on a daily basis. According to the 2009 National School Climate Survey of the Gay, Lesbian & Straight Education Network (GLSEN), 72.4% of students reported hearing derogatory language such as "faggot" and "dyke" (Kosciw, Greytak, Diaz, & Bartkiewicz, 2010). In the same report, 40.1% of students reported physical harassment because of their sexual orientation while 27.2% experienced physical harassment because of their gender orientation (Kosciw et al., 2010). Physical assault on the basis of sexual orientation was reported by 18.8% of the students, and 12.5% reported physical assault because of their gender identity (Kosciw et al., 2010). Students also reported that they were more likely to hear homophobic comments in the presence of teachers than other forms of biased comments.

In the 2007 National School Climate Survey of the Gay, Lesbian & Straight Education Network, Kevin Jennings, then-executive director of GLSEN, expressed his frustration with the lack of improvement since the surveys began in 1999:

> I quite honestly feel a little depressed by how little things have improved from when we published our first report almost a decade ago. Why is it—when research shows so clearly that there are specific policy and programmatic interventions that will make our schools safer—that so many states and districts do nothing, allowing schools to remain an unsafe space for so many LGBTQ students? (quoted in Kosciw, Diaz, & Greytak, 2007, p. viii)

Robinson, Espelage, and Rivers (2013) do find that experiences of harassment diminish over time but still point to differences in experiences between genders and sexualities that require school interventions. Robinson and Espelage (2012) find, too, that bullying only explains some of the disparities in risk factors of LGBTQ youth compared to heterosexual youth and warn that only by focusing on bullying, schools will miss other possibilities for improving the lives of LGBTQ youth.

INTERSECTING HARASSMENTS AND BIASES

In the 2009 GLSEN National School Climate Survey, researchers found that White, Latina/o, and multiracial LGBTQ students felt more unsafe at school compared to Black or Asian students. Multiracial students also report higher levels of harassment and assault based on sexual orientation and on gender expression than do other racial groups. Transgender students report feeling more unsafe at school because of gender identity and because of sexual orientation than do male or female students (Kosciw et al., 2010). This experience of feeling unsafe at school also extends to young women in general. According to an American Association of University Women (2001) study, 83% of young women experience sexual harassment, and 20% of them avoid school or certain classes in order to stay away from their tormentors. Young lesbians, gender nonconforming young women, and any young person who is deemed by a harasser to be acting in gender inappropriate ways—including turning down sexual interest—may all be targets for homophobic and sexist harassment.

The relationship among gender bias, homophobia, and harassment is complicated. On the one hand, young women of all sexualities experience harassment, including homophobic harassment if they act in ways that do not fit the norms for women. So the scope of gender and sexuality–related harassment is quite broad for women. Because young men have a narrower range of acceptable masculine behavior, they too are targets for homophobic harassment on the basis of any gender nonconforming behavior, including having any forms of disagreement devolve into homophobic taunts. The intersections of categories of identity, then, must become central to how educators think and learn before they can begin to teach their students. These complex intersections of identity categories also extend to those of race, ethnicity, gender, and sexuality. The 2005 GLSEN National School Climate Survey reported these findings:

> It appears that students most often report being targeted for verbal harassment based on multiple characteristics (e.g., being gay and Latino) or perhaps on the intersections of these characteristics (e.g., being a gay Latino). With regard to the more extreme forms of victimization, physical harassment and assault, it appears that sexual orientation alone becomes more salient. For example, the largest number of students of color reported being verbally harassed because of both their sexual orientation and race/ethnicity, followed by sexual orientation only (44.4% and 35.7%, respectively). However, nearly twice as many students of color reported physical assault because of their sexual orientation alone than reported assault because of both race/ethnicity and sexual orientation (11.7% vs. 6.8%). (Kosciw & Diaz, 2005, p. 62)

As Francisco Galarte (2012) explains in an article on *The Feminist Wire*, thinking about violence against trangender people of color too often is discussed only as an indication of transphobia or homophobia. He argues that this analysis misses the centrality of racism:

> It is racism that animates transphobia and homophobia as seen in the increasingly violent iterations of violence toward trans* people of color. Brown trans* bodies are a threat to racialized, sexualized, and gendered dominance. These bodies are simultaneously much too seen and not seen at all. Moreover, racialized, sexualized, and gendered violence, as an instrument of sociopolitical terrorism and control, has been increasingly normalized so that the policing, punishment, and subjugation of certain bodies (namely racialized and gendered bodies) go unnoticed.

His analysis, like that of Paceley and Flynn (2012), questions the neglect of concern about violence against LGBTQ people and youth of color in the mass media. By centralizing race as the key component in such violence, analyses like Galarte's and Vivian Namaste's (2009) also push us to think about the relationship between racial discrimination and social status, including the forms of employment open to young transgender people, especially youth of color, pushed out of schools and homes.

While most LGBTQ youth flourish and learn to counter the homophobic challenges they face, and while it is important not only to focus on the challenges but also to stress the strength and resiliency of all minority youth, it is also crucial to understand that the costs of homophobia and bias against gender nonconforming students, especially those contending with racism or other intersecting differences, can be very high. In February 2008, 15-year-old Lawrence King was murdered by a younger White student who had been part of a group bullying him for most of the school year. King endured daily taunting. King's 12-year-old friend Erin Mings said, "What he did was really brave—to wear makeup and high-heeled boots." Mings hung out with King at E. O. Green Junior High School. "Every corner he turned around, people were saying, 'Oh, my God, he's wearing makeup today.'" Mings said King stood his ground and was an outgoing and funny boy. "When people came up and started punking him, he just stood up for himself" (Saillant, 2008a).

Lawrence King's story underscores the strength of young gender nonconforming gay people, their sense of confidence about their identity, and as well, the very real dangers they can face in public schools. Wearing eye shadow to school and trying to be himself in this hostile context of school, Larry was continually open to taunting and bullying and tried to keep strong by flirting with his tormentors (Saillant, 2008b). Reports indicate that school officials were aware of the potential difficulties between Larry and his attacker but did not intervene (Saillant, 2008b).

King's story not only demonstrates his energy and commitment to living his life, it also stands as a reminder that much homophobia is fueled by bias against gender nonconformity. The Gender Public Advocacy Coalition (Gender PAC), an organization that was active from 1995 to 2009, was dedicated to educating about gender identity. It noted in its 2002 annual report that not only were gender nonconforming students the victims of bullying but also students who engaged in school violence had experienced such bullying: "five of eight assailants in recent school shooting incidents were reportedly students who had been repeatedly gender-bashed and gender-baited in school" (Gender PAC, 2002, p. 8). An American Association of University Women (2001) study reported that more than almost anything else, students do not want to be called gay or lesbian; 74% said they would be very upset, understanding the cultural pressures to be heterosexual and the potential harassment that affects LGBTQ youth.

Even students who are not gay report overt homophobic and sexual harassment when they express support for sexual minorities. As one student put it, after experiencing sexualized death threats from other students while teachers did nothing to stop them, "Maybe it's because I have strong views. I've always spoken out for gays and lesbians, for Latinos, for those who get trampled on in our society. Still, I really have no idea why I was treated with such hostility" (Ruenzel, 1999, p. 24). The pressure on straight allies of LGBTQ students to not express their opposition to homophobia may indicate that not supporting gay people is an integral part of indicating one's own heterosexuality. Like Sleeter's (1994) observations that White people perform their race by expressing racist attitudes, people may perform heterosexuality by indicating their dislike of or discomfort around homosexuality.

The pressure on all students to conform to a gendered or heterosexual norm is powerful, especially in the school context where public knowledge and choices about identity are closely watched (Thorne, 1993). The public context of 15-year-old Black gender nonconforming Sakia Gunn's assertion of her lesbianism when sexually and homophobically harassed on a street in Newark, New Jersey, was both an important assertion of her claiming space in her community and the occasion of her murder by her harasser ("Lesbian Stabbing," 2003). Her space of assertion was honored by the Newark community's outcry against homophobic violence in a mass vigil commemorating Gunn's death and life (Smothers, 2004). A year after her killing, the school district that refused to have a moment of silence for her immediately after her murder allowed the anniversary to be acknowledged by having "No Name Calling Day" (Smothers, 2004). It is important to understand that homophobic violence and the potential for harassment do structure the lives of sexual minorities. But the understanding of their identities, of the places to go to find communities that support their gender and sexual identities, and of their ability to express their identities—even in challenging situations—demonstrates that sexual and gender minority youth like Gunn are actively and creatively involved in making their lives and communities. Indeed, Galarte (2012) warns that by only giving attention to gender nonconforming people of color when they are murdered, we "limit the ability to which trans* persons of color can imagine themselves as not always already dead," but nonetheless such violence must be recognized.

There has been much coverage of the role of the Internet in the harassment that led to Tyler Clementi's suicide after his first sexual experience with another man was recorded without his knowledge by his roommate and circulated on the Internet. Cyberbullying adds to the other forms of harassment LGBTQ youth, as well as any youth, face. But the Internet, as Chapter 6 examines in more depth, can also provide support, as can educational lessons on how to navigate and critique technology-based communication and social media sites. The "It Gets Better Project," also Internet-based, provides short videos of LGBT and ally adults reassuring young people that there are adults out there who are supportive or who themselves went through homophobic bullying. Showing young people that there are a wide number of prominent and caring people who want to see them succeed and provide them with information on bullying hotlines and LGBT advocacy organizations may be one way to help work against the isolation they experience.

LGBTQ YOUTH AND THE CHALLENGES OF ACCESSING EDUCATION

The examples of youth suicide or homophobic and transphobic murder are extreme manifestations of bias. But in each case, a less spectacular, more everyday experience of homophobia or transphobia also preceded the more violent act. In other words, these were students who were already making their way through school contexts that were not supportive and did not take seriously their concerns about peer or adult bias. That kind of isolation or harassment, in and of itself, has a negative impact on school attendance and educational aspirations of many LGBTQ students. GLSEN's *2011 National School Climate Survey* (Kosciw, Greytak, Bartkiewicz, Boesen, & Palmer, 2012) includes some relevant findings. For example, LGBTQ students who experience extreme harassment in schools are twice as likely to report no plans to continue their education beyond high school, and students who experienced more LGBTQ-related victimization at schools reported a lower grade point average. In addition, the level of severity of harassment and assault was related to lower rates of school attendance. Further, youth who are out or public about their gender identity or sexual orientation were more likely to also report experiencing more harassment, but they also expressed a higher sense of self-esteem.

Despite what sometimes seems to be an overwhelmingly hostile context in schools, the concerted efforts of students, teachers, administrators, and other members of the school community can shift school climates. As the GLSEN 2009 survey (Kosciw et al., 2010) shows, schools can make a difference in the experiences of LGBTQ youth. For example, students in schools with Gay-Straight Alliances report hearing fewer homophobic remarks, report seeing staff intervene in bias more often, and were less likely to feel unsafe in their schools. Moreover, students in schools with inclusive curriculum reported lower levels of harassment, higher attendance rates, and more feelings of connection to their schools. However, progress can be undone without adequate institutional and teacher support. Teachers themselves may find it difficult in some contexts to advocate for LGBTQ students either because they themselves do not want to be outed or because they are concerned they will be misrecognized as LGBTQ because of their advocacy. One of the first Gay-Straight Alliances to attain the right to meet in public schools using the federal Equal Access Act disbanded years later because of continuing community hostility and lack of institutional advocacy and support. That group, however, was recently reorganized and supported by a unanimous vote by school officials who had been educated about and were now supportive of anti-homophobia projects (American Civil Liberties Union, 2006).

Students' health and risk behaviors are also affected by homophobic and transphobic experiences at school. Negative experiences at school involving gender identity or anti-gay harassment can include depression, stress, anxiety, and consideration of suicide (D'Augelli, Grossman, & Starks, 2006; Williams et al., 2005). Students who feel unsafe at school or unconnected to school because they have no support for their experiences of homophobia and transphobia may engage in unsafe sexual behavior and substance abuse (Bontempo & D'Augelli, 2002). LGBTQ students may not only lack support at school, they may also face rejection from their families with a similar outcome of greater risk for thoughts of suicide, unsafe sexual behavior, and substance abuse (Grossman & D'Augelli, 2006; C. C. Ryan, Huebner, Diaz, & Sanchez, 2009). Thinking about the obstacles faced by LGBTQ youth, who experience a wide range of exclusions in their attempts to access education, may help provide a better school-based response to ensure their educational success. In addition, because LGBTQ youth may not find support at home, school-based support and advocacy for their access to education is all the more crucial.

RESITUATING "BULLYING" IN SEXUAL HARASSMENT

The topic of bullying has gotten much media coverage and school-based attention in the last several years. But *bullying* as a term does not capture the institutional scope of exclusion that LGBTQ and other minority youth experience. Nor does the term *bullying* itself necessarily encourage school personnel to think broadly about exclusionary and hostile experiences students face, especially those that are based on gender and sexual orientation. Indeed, researchers on bullying caution that misunderstandings about the relationship between bullying and institutional, pervasive bias miss not only the rights-based aspects of gender-based bias, but miss as well the damaging effects of such experiences. Nan Stein (2003) cites a Vermont case where a young, middle school boy was harassed by students who thought he was gay. His parents, using a then-new Vermont law on bullying, took the case to court and lost, although had the case been based on a federal Title IX claim rather than a state anti-bullying law, they would likely have been successful. Stein argues that in the rush to provide for school safety after Columbine and in a climate of continuing attention to bullying, schools have adopted rules that "de-gender" school-based harassment, in effect, leading them to also neglect existing federal protections for students (p. 787). Relatedly, school districts have not provided enough training for school professionals on their legal obligations to protect students' rights, and additionally, the discourse of bullying has shifted focus away from rights and onto the figure of the bully, an individualized, seemingly isolated cause of school problems (Stein, 2003).

Such misunderstandings of law and policy lead to category errors in enforcement or to ignoring the problem of harassment altogether. In their examination of how teachers understand anti-bullying and anti-sexual harassment laws, Charmaraman, Jones, Stein, and Espelage (2013) found that teachers believed bullying to refer to unpleasant peer-to-peer relationships but did not understand that sexual harassment could be peer-based. Further, teachers did not connect what they took to be boys bullying girls with Title IX's prohibition of hostile gender-based environment created by sexual harassment. Charmaraman et al. argue that more training is needed to ensure that school professionals understand Title IX's requirement that policies and action ensure an equitable learning environment. As discussed in the introduction to this volume, neglecting to protect students from gender-based discrimination can lead to school district liability, as well as negative student outcomes, so ensuring that all school personnel understand their obligations is crucial. Charmaraman et al. (2013) also found that school personnel were inadequately trained to access already-existing school-based resources on bullying and Title IX and were unaware of negative psychological and health-related outcomes related to experiences of bias in schools.

The impact of these misunderstandings can have a major effect on students' ability to access education and to thrive in school and out. James E. Gruber and Susan Fineran (2008) found that the adverse effects of sexual harassment were greater than those of bullying and those adverse effects were particularly evident among young women and sexual minority students. Boys, too, they found were more significantly affected by sexual harassment than by bullying. Gruber and Fineran conclude that if schools are seriously interested in safety for all students, but especially young women and gay, lesbian, bisexual and questioning students, they need to return to emphasizing sexual harassment prevention:

We are not suggesting that bullying prevention programs be curtailed; rather, we would argue that sexual harassment prevention receive attention as a distinct focus. All students need to benefit from a safe school environment and the mental and physical health implications from sexual harassment and bullying behaviors need to be considered. Keeping schools safe in the twenty-first century is a worthy goal but continuing to focus on boys' behavior and bullying violence in schools, rather than on all students' negative experiences with sexual harassment detracts from our ability to provide a healthy environment for all children. (p. 13)

School climates that allow sexual harassment and bullying to continue have a negative impact on all students, whether through the general discomfort of being around hostility, the particular message of intolerance extending beyond those to whom it is directed, or simply the fact that very narrow understandings of sexuality and gender are broadcast through the school without interruption (Payne & Smith, 2012). Such heteronormative environments affect everyone, even pushing heterosexual-identified students to express their anxieties about homosexuality and potential for misidentification of their sexuality (AAUW, 2001; Pascoe, 2007). Certainly the experience of hostility and disapproval has an effect on LGBTQ youth school outcomes. In addition, research indicates that such negative outcomes to school-based bias are felt even more strongly by students who are questioning their sexuality (Williams et al., 2005). Finding neither overt support from LGBTQ youth, because they either haven't joined such friendship or organizational networks or because they do not fit the definitions of the terms LGBTQ, nor finding support from heterosexual peers because they don't fit there either, questioning youth are isolated and experience more bullying and depression (Birkett, Espelage, & Koenig, 2008).

But teachers feel pressured to maintain their focus on accountability and also report not feeling well prepared to address incidents of harassment (Lichty, Torres, Valenti, & Buchanan, 2008; Meyer, 2008). Teachers further report that they themselves are not well prepared on issues related to LGBTQ students (Meyer, 2008; Sears, 1992). Even teachers who know they should be proactive in challenging homophobia find themselves unable to go against social and institutional pressures (Sears, 1992).

This research on the disconnection between policies and school action points to a number of different challenges for teacher and administrator preparation programs. We need to find ways to motivate those teachers and leaders who are already aware of the need for advocacy, but are not able to overcome their personal biases or overcome the obstacles that other people's biases pose for them. In addition, preservice teachers and administrators who want to be better practitioners need to know the scope of the problems facing LGBTQ youth in schools, the laws and regulations that can help them improve school climate, and how to put their knowledge into practice. Homophobia and transphobia, in a very real sense, affect everyone—even professionals who know they ought to do better by sexual and gender minority students feel constrained by it, and those who have not yet been educated about those issues have experienced that neglect because of the same forms of bias.

These examples point to the need to address homophobia and sexual minority issues through multilevel approaches. Youth are capable of asserting themselves and finding community with others, but without the institutional support of schools and the interventions of respectful adults, the struggles they may have to face are all the more daunting. Ensuring that sexual minority and gender minority identity youth have space and time to meet together creates one space in school that addresses their communities. Incorporating LGBTQ and gender identity issues in curricula, teacher education, school leadership programs, and school anti-discrimination policies are all strategies that reinforce inclusion across the entire school institution.

ANOTHER FORM OF "NOT" EDUCATION: "YOU CAN'T SAY GAY" POLICIES

Each of these steps requires more than just stopping harassment. It requires thinking critically about the messages in curricula, the way teachers and administrators talk to students, and the way school-based social events are organized. Exclusions of LGBTQ-related information signal to students that such people are not respected members of the school community, and into the vacuum of official school silence bias from students can go unchallenged. In the Anoka Hennepin district of suburban Minneapolis, school policy required that teachers maintain neutrality on the topic of homosexuality, until it was revised in light of a successful court challenge. Purportedly concerned that teacher authority can be coercive on sensitive topics, the district developed a policy that would require teachers to not respond to questions about sexual orientation or offer their own opinions on LGBTQ issues. The number of suicides of LGBTQ students, bullied in schools using this policy, led to parents and students to organize and challenge it. Teachers were positioned as authority figures who ought not to express their own position on the issue while students were allowed to continue to shape the school environment in ways that let at least some opinions on homosexuality circulate freely. According to some parents, including the mothers of two students whose experiences of homophobic harassment contributed to their suicides (two of four suicides related to sexuality or perceived sexuality in that school district), the school itself was not neutral; indeed it became more hostile toward their children. Parents and LGBTQ and ally students argued, too, that when authority figures in schools retreated from contentious issues, students with strong—and mostly negative—opinions filled the gaps.

Part of the difficulty with the policy was the assumption that if teachers were neutral, the school experience would reflect that neutrality; another related problem was that positive education about sexuality and gender stopped (Mayo, 2013). The tactic message to students who see that teachers do not intervene in homophobic harassment may be that such acts are acceptable, not only in the school but in the broader community, and that no authority figure will provide LGBTQ students and their allies with support. According to a recent GLSEN survey of school environment (Kosciw et al., 2010), 33.8% of school personnel surveyed did nothing in response to students who reported anti-LGBTQ incidents to them. Close to 25% of the faculty or staff confronted the student(s) accused of anti-LGBTQ bullying and harassment, and 20% of them punished the accused students. Students who attended schools that intervened in anti-LGBTQ harassment and who also had supportive faculty reported better attendance rates and school success. Teachers in the Anoka Hennepin district themselves recognized the problem with the policy of neutrality imposed there, not only because of its intent to keep them neutral but also because the extent of their necessary neutrality was unclear. This lack of clarity, some argued, meant that many teachers were overcautious in taking any action against homophobic bullying, wondering, "Could I get fired for that?" (Wooledge, 2012). Anoka High School teacher Mary Jo Merrick-Lockett explained, "If you can't talk about it in any context, which is how teachers interpret district policies, kids internalize that to mean that being gay must be so shameful and wrong. . . . And that has created a climate of fear and repression and harassment" (quoted in Erdely, 2012). By restricting teachers to neutrality, then, the policy created a hostile environment in the school.

As national media attention became focused on the policy, the board decided to replace it with a policy that would have required teachers to remain neutral not only on issues of sexual orientation, but on all so-called controversial issues. Yet the impending lawsuit and eventual settlement squashed that even broader attempt at defining *neutrality* in terms of teacher disengagement (Erdely, 2012). The Anoka-Hennepin school district has since settled a lawsuit brought by students in the district, the Southern Poverty Law Center, and the National Center for Lesbian Rights. In agreeing to the consent decree, the district has replaced its "neutrality" policy with a multitiered approach to addressing harassment based on sexual orientation and gender identity. According to the consent decree negotiated between the U.S. Office of Civil Rights, the students and the district, the district now must take proactive steps to ensure that students' rights under Title IX and the Fourteenth Amendment, as well as Minnesota's Human Rights law, are protected. The consent decree states that "all harassment, including that based on nonconformity to gender stereotypes and/or gender identity and expression," (8) as well as any "sex-based or sexual orientation-based," (10) is prohibited. All school personnel receiving a report of such harassment need to "investigate, address, and respond" to such reports following all relevant laws and regulations (9) (*Doe v. Anoka Hennepin*, 2012).

RECOGNIZING FAMILY DIVERSITY:
LGBTQ-HEADED HOUSEHOLDS AND SCHOOL EXCLUSION

Harassment and exclusion based on homophobia and transphobia also extends to families, including families of LGBTQ youth or families whose members are LGBTQ (Casper & Schultz, 1999). Increasingly, LGBTQ families are involved in their children's education or interested in advocating for LGBTQ youth and do not always find schools supportive of their concerns. Given the now 30% of the U.S. population living in states where same-sex marriage is legal, schools need to be more responsive to this historic time for the growth—and public representation—of families who are either LGBTQ headed or who are actively involved in ensuring that schools respectfully educate their LGBTQ children. Difficulties remain however, as most states still have laws or state constitutions outlawing same-sex marriage. As one gay male parent explains, "I still carry the adoption paper with me in my wallet just in case I'm ever stopped" (Wells, 2011, p. 167), knowing full well that single men with children, especially gay men, are still culturally suspect.

The most recent U.S. Census in 2010 reported over 900,000 same-sex couples. Other estimates put the number of gay families between 1.4 and 14 million. There is no especially reliable way to get a baseline number of how many families are LGBTQ headed, have LGBTQ members, or have LGBTQ children, but there is a clear indication that LGBTQ families are there and want schools to be responsive to their concerns. Perhaps related to cultural norms indicating a link between "marriage" and children, same-sex couples are more likely to define themselves as "married" if they have children, whether or not they live in a state where same-sex marriage is legal (Lofquist, 2012). In other words, children and marriage seem to go together in same-sex headed households, and same-sex headed households increasingly expect that schools will recognize them as such, even if their experience may lead them to also expect resistance or ignorance from school personnel. Given other forms of family diversity, whether single-parent families, adoptive families, blended, and/or multigenerational families, LGBTQ families should be represented as one of many caring options that a child might aspire to join or might already be living in. But teachers themselves indicate challenges to including LGBTQ families in their lessons, voicing concerns that they will offend conservative parents or bring "sex" into the classroom (Martino & Cumming-Potvin, 2011). To complicate the potential controversy around same-sex headed households, teacher education programs generally do not yet spend adequate time preparing preservice teachers to think carefully about the implications of forms that indicate a mother and father need to sign—an issue as important for children in same-sex households as it is for a variety of other family types including single parent, grandparent-headed, adoptive, blended, or multigenerational families—or to be welcoming when two same-sex partners come to parent–teacher conferences. If teachers are not adequately prepared to look for diverse family representation, they may exacerbate the feelings of exclusion that children from diverse family structures already experience from the exclusion that may be represented in storybooks or textbooks. Children from same-sex headed households report a similar level of homophobic harassment as do LGBTQ youth and represent yet another way that pervasive homophobia affects more than LGBTQ people. In addition, children from same-sex headed households share another commonality with LGBTQ youth who do not feel comfortable sharing their experiences of harassment with parents: For children of same-sex parents, a concern that the parents will blame themselves for the harassment their children suffer can mean that young people are reluctant to tell their parents (Welsh, 2011). Further, because children of same-sex parents feel that they need to be exemplars, in a sense acting as proof that young people can and do thrive in LGBTQ-headed households, they are reluctant to share with anyone that they are experiencing difficulties, even if those difficulties are the result of homophobia and not their family structure per se (Welsh, 2011).

Cultural support for diverse families, including LGBTQ families, is changing, of course. Every year another state or locality recognizes same-sex marriage and still debates over including constitutional amendments in various state constitutions are also ongoing. While recent Supreme Court rulings have made some headway toward marriage equality, in some ways they have created even more national confusion. Married couples in states that have legalized same-sex marriage or have laws recognizing same-sex marriages performed in other states are now able to access over a thousand federal benefits associated with marriage. Same-sex couples in all other states likely remain unable to access state or federal benefits even if they have lived in and were married in states that allowed same-sex marriage. Even with continued progress toward marriage equality in legislatures and referenda, the cultural debate over diverse families, especially LGBTQ families, will likely not be settled soon—or given the pace of cultural change, perhaps it will. The point here is that there is still at the moment of writing this, uncertainty about what the changes in some states and some national policy will bring. Will cultural change now move more quickly? Will marriage continue to be the benchmark for LGBTQ equality and if so, what sorts of exclusions and normative assumptions come with that linkage? Will work on marriage equality enable further progress on access to equality for transpeople and others for whom marriage does not represent a goal or a solution to their experiences of exclusion? Whether other laws restricting same-sex marriage will soon be invalidated or whether the cultural dispute over same-sex marriage continues, understanding more about how to rethink teaching about diverse families, sexualities, and gender identities is another way to challenge the negative school-based experiences of LGBTQ people. At the same time, though, marriage is not the only issue that concerns people of diverse sexualities and gender identities, so a discussion of the legal cases defining and expanding marriage is not meant to indicate this is the only issue that affects LGBTQ people.

LIVING IN FAMILIES UNDER PUBLIC DEBATE: LEGAL AND SOCIAL CONTEXTS

Understanding that not only are LGBT issues under cultural debate but they are framed by laws that set the context for young people's self-understanding may help us understand how crucial schools are to helping provide support for young people who may feel under attack not only from school bullies and parental disapproval but also from popular opinion and government decisions. When Section 3 of the Defense of Marriage Act (DOMA), enacted in 1996, was found unconstitutional by the Supreme Court in 2013, one blogger described how the debates around it and same-sex marriage had led her 1st-grade daughter and her daughter's friends to fear that legal changes would threaten her family:

> The kids' friends were supportive, too. Both of them had a friend use the same word—"stupid"—to describe the fact that gay marriage wasn't legal (before it was in Maryland). It was harder for June's friends (and June herself) to grasp the legal details of it all and what was really at stake. In fact, last fall June's friend Talia thought that if the argument was about whether or not gay marriage should be legal, that meant if the vote went the wrong way, Beth and I might be carted off to jail for being illegally married, and she was quite concerned about who would take care of June. Around that same time June was worried that the four of us might not be allowed to live together after the election.
>
> We re-assured her and we thought she understood, but when the DOMA vote came up, she worried all over again that we might all be doing something illegal in living our lives. And even though we explained that everything would be fine no matter how the election or court decision went, in a way, she and Talia hit on a core truth of the matter—it *was* about whether our lives are seen as legitimate. It's a hard lesson for a seven-year-old to learn, that not everyone looks at her family and sees a family. So that's another reason the decision is a relief. It will give June a sense of security. (Steph, 2013)

As this blog about a 1st-grader and her friends trying to understand the political debate around same-sex marriage shows, young people are both very aware of changes around them and not always completely certain about what they mean. It is not surprising then that these larger political debates also wind their way into school lessons and student interactions. For some LGBTQ students, the only representation they see in their schools are the yearly staged debates in current events class about whether same-sex marriage should be legal or not, debates that seem to allow homophobic students a legitimate place to voice their disapproval of homosexuality.

Understanding more details about how these changes have happened, but are still up for debate, may help explain how tentative parents of LGBTQ youth feel their relationship to social institutions is or how vigorously they are willing to work in order to ensure that educational institutions respond to their family's needs. In a relatively short period of time, the Constitution has gone from being interpreted to allow restrictions on same-sex sexuality to overturning that decision and instead finding that intimate relationships have Constitutional protections. In 1986 in *Bowers v. Hardwick*, the Supreme Court found that laws against sodomy between consenting adults of the same sex were Constitutional, noting that other cases that had broadened privacy rights for relationships involved forms of relationship closely related to conventional families. The decision, too, dismissed as ridiculous any idea that same-sex sexuality could be protected by the Constitution, given the long history of disapproval.

In 2003, overturning *Bowers v. Hardwick*, the Supreme Court found in *Lawrence v. Texas* that the right to same-sex sodomy is not ridiculous, but instead argued that the earlier court had dramatically underestimated the relationship between sexual relationships, privacy, and the need for people to determine their own intimate bonds with one another. Sexuality, it found, was part of what kept people together and enabled relationships to flourish. While *Lawrence* has had an overwhelmingly positive effect on the lives of many gay people, bringing to end sodomy laws between consenting adults that were not only used to restrict sexual behavior but were also used to deny child custody, prohibit public school curricula on LGBTQ issues, and justify discriminatory practices in employment, nonetheless by linking sexual activity to family-like commitment, the justification for giving protection and recognition to same-sex couples hinges on their similarities with reproductive heterosexual couples (Landau, 2003). The growing respect for gay and lesbian families, and the link between same-sex marriage rights and ensuring the support for children, is even clearer in the *Goodridge v. Dept. of Public Health* decision. Despite its opening statements confirming that marriage is not an institution for procreation alone, the decision does suggest that gay people have rights because they have children and that it is the children who most need to be protected from laws that discriminate against their parents.

Schools, too, need to encourage forms of association that make diverse life choices possible for students. Marriage is not the only form of intimate relationship in which one finds the best expressions of one's autonomy. There is also friendship, association, and other forms of intimate relation that do not entail a particular sort of ceremony. But given the larger cultural dispute over whether same-sex marriage should be allowed, even when more than a dozen states, adding up to a significant percentage of the U.S. population, give that right, same-sex marriage rights are an important indication of whether or not a state and the people living in it are inclined to discriminate against sexual minorities. The larger context and meaning of such laws, while not definitively guaranteeing particular experiences, do send a message about such contexts, much like schools send messages about the kind of respectful behavior expected when they enact, educate about, and implement nondiscrimination policies.

Same-sex marriage rights also help schools ensure that diverse students and families are respected and represented by curricula. But if we think of schools and their representation of diverse families as related to helping people live well in their communities, same-sex marriage laws in and of themselves do not address all inequities that people of diverse sexualities and genders experience. While many people have deep personal motivations to enjoy the benefits that accrue to being legally married couples, the issue of inequalities in health care provision is not solved by providing benefits only to those in committed and civilly unionized relationships. Nor do same-sex marriage rights in and of themselves solve the discrimination that gender nonconforming people face or that people who choose not to marry also face. In addition, given the patchwork of employment and housing protections based on sexual orientation and gender identity, marriage rights on their own do not solve a wide range of inequalities.

Nor have same-sex marriage cases yet squarely addressed the fundamental rights that LGBTQ people are unable to access, even with marriage reform. Decisions do, however, provide insight into what state and federal responsibilities are in terms of marriage and why it is a secular institution under the purview of state laws, and now also not subject to discrimination on the basis of federal laws. For instance, the Massachusetts Supreme Judicial Court found in *Goodridge v. Dept. of Public Health* (2003) that the state has no compelling reason to rely on religious definitions of marriage. While supporters of same-sex marriage had hoped this case would set a precedent for sexual minorities having protection as a suspect class or having broader rights reinforced by considering their right to equal protection under the law where attempts to limit their freedom would have necessitated strict scrutiny from courts, this was denied in the *Goodridge* ruling and avoided again when the Supreme Court returned Proposition 8 to California courts. The court found that the state's lack of rational basis in prohibiting same-sex marriage was enough for it to countermand state regulations and that the case did not demand the higher standard of strict scrutiny. So even in this moment where a court decision clearly upsets common-sense understandings of who can legitimately be considered a family, it nonetheless did not see the restriction on marriage as a violation of a fundamental right. The Supreme Court in *United States v. Windsor* (2013), finding Section 3 of the *Defense of Marriage Act* to be unconstitutional, continues to both assert the importance of marriage for gay and lesbian couples but has yet to definitively call for marriage equality, instead leaving the issue of regulation of marriage to the states. In *Hollingsworth v. Perry* (2013), the Supreme Court potentially creates more vexing challenges, even as it returns the issue of same-sex marriage to the lower court that had already overturned Proposition 8's outlawing of same-sex marriage as against the California constitution. The Supreme Court ruled only on the lack of standing of those who wanted to see Proposition 8 enforced, not on the relationship between marriage rights and equal rights. The California Supreme Court and the United States District Court each have held that Proposition 8 violated the Fourteenth Amendment's guarantee of due process and equal protection of the law in its outlawing of same-sex marriage.

Such distinctions about fundamental rights are important for the continuing attempts to broaden same-sex marriage rights but there are other effects of legal changes, whatever their particular grounding. Having legalized same-sex marriage, Massachusetts was able to not only extend civil rights more broadly to LGBTQ people, but also to justify including curriculum supporting diverse families and lessons on LGBTQ issues into schools. This link between public schools and same-sex marriage has also stimulated opposition among those who disagree with same-sex marriage and disagree that schools have any place in supporting LGBTQ youth. Kilman (2012) reported that opposition to gay teachers seemed to increase in response to this change in laws. In addition, the Parkers, a family who felt their son was being forced to read about the potential for same-sex romance in *King and King*, a children's book about a young prince who doesn't like girls and instead chooses another prince as his potential mate, argued that their religious freedom was violated by curricular changes after the legalization of same-sex marriage (United States District Court, *Parker v. Hurley*, 2007).

The simple point is that in states where same-sex marriage is legal, school districts find it easier to support teaching about LGBTQ issues and teaching about diverse families. While public debate may continue and religious beliefs may differ, laws provide schools with guidance on curriculum and nondiscrimination policies, helping them broaden curricular coverage, as California has in adding LGBTQ history to its high school curriculum, or including readings on diverse families to elementary students as Massachusetts and other states have. But like the blog about June shows, living under continuing social debate is stressful, and research on gay male health has also shown a relationship between risk activities and such political debates (White & Stephenson, 2013).

CHAPTER 4

Educatively Addressing
LGBTQ Issues

This chapter examines strategies and projects for including LGBTQ-related issues in schools in educative ways, the implications for critical analysis of sexual
and gendered norms for all, and the need to engage bias with more education,
instead of punitive responses. In contrast to zero tolerance programs, briefly ana-
lyzed here, I argue that using pedagogical strategies and curricular goals to more
effectively educate about and against homophobic and transphobic harassment,
as well as racism, classism, and sexism in schools, can help challenge the persistent silences discussed in the previous chapter. In addition, educating about
the persistence of homophobia and heterosexism can give students a fuller sense
of why certain varieties of prejudice have wide circulation and implications that
stretch beyond their purported targets. Further, by engaging such processes in
more detail, students and the broader school community are more fully equipped
to understand how homophobia and heterosexism have structured their own
learning experience and how curiosities, doubt, fantasy, uncertainty and questions about sexual orientation and gender identity are part of everyone's experience. Drawing on pedagogical suggestions from a variety of academic areas, this
chapter not only provides concrete strategies as well as theoretical discussion for
these interventions but also suggests that our educational approaches to LGBTQ
issues have to stay a source of difficulty (Britzman, 1995; Kumashiro, 2002).
Identity, community, and relationships related to sexual and gender identity are
not only historically and politically complex, by engaging forms of desire, their
meanings and practices are not completely knowable. As we attempt to make
such issues part of schooling, then, we need to be aware that the queerness of
sexuality, not just in regard to LGBTQ issues, will continue to generate new possibilities, uncertainties and tensions.

ZERO TOLERANCE AND EXACERBATING DISTANCE

LGBTQ-related education should expand beyond risk, bias, and harassment,
though addressing those is also important. School-based anti-homophobia and

anti-transphobia interventions are impeded by zero tolerance rules that punish offending students without responding to the social and school context that frames and prepares bias. Such policies shut down education in favor of stopping an incident—not an unreasonable goal—but because they may be punitive without creating an opportunity to teach or to rethink how the school climate has been shaped by exclusion, systemic change may not follow—and certainly understanding of the place of gender and sexuality in everyone's experiences does not follow. When framed in terms of focusing on bias and punishment, intolerance is understood only as an individual act and not as a pervasive atmosphere of exclusion that enables or even encourages such individual acts. Even more educationally based approaches to anti-homophobia and anti-transphobia education may reinforce the distance between those who need to be personally concerned about being targets of such bias and other people who just need to be aware that it happens. Anti-bias pedagogies, in other words, reinforce the distance between members of a minority group and those of the majority, as if gender, sexuality, and pressure to be normal weren't structuring features of everyone's lives. Pedagogies aimed at reducing bias may also address differences in piecemeal fashion, stressing sexual orientation without referencing its relationship to other aspects of identity and community, like gender, gender identity, race, language, ethnicity, religion, and social class.

Not only does keeping all of these complications part of providing support for LGBTQ and ally students help make apparent the multiple ways in which homophobia, transphobia, and other biases structure common understandings of categories and expectations for behavior and relationship, but these complications can also help raise questions about norms in general. In other words, providing for critical reflection on why certain identities and communities are respected and others are reviled and harassed opens a larger question about power imbalances, as well as making the intersections among identity categories more apparent. But even this list of do's and don'ts doesn't get to the difficulties of rethinking both the intransigent persistence of bias and the constant presence of non-normative critique. Nor do the various stipulations get to how hard it is to rethink categories by which we know ourselves and others, let alone how much we may rely on our tendencies to ignore differences we desire or differences that repel us or those that do both.

These are not easy tasks and pedagogy is not an easy process so schools may simply decide to avoid teaching and aim only at punishment when addressing LGBTQ issues. By only focusing on punishment and prohibition, learning is discouraged. Further, thinking and teaching about LGBTQ issues only in the context of bias-related incidents reinforces the idea that LGBTQ students are only noticeable when they are threatened or only recognized as present when they are fully out in conventional ways. Thinking about pedagogies to address bias and to welcome difference means changing the reactive framework, moving teachers back into learning mode along with students. Nelson Rodriguez (2007) has suggested that encouraging heterosexual teachers to queer themselves, to think about the disruptions of sexuality occasioned by gay rights and queer popular media representations can help teachers work with LGBTQ students, and all other students as well, on these issues. Work like this carries on the tradition of Martin Rochlin's (1972) "Heterosexual Questionnaire" that reversed the usual questions asked to gays and lesbians about coming out, telling their families, and talking to friends about sexuality. Rochlin's tactic of asking heterosexuals when they came out and how their friends and family reacted to their heterosexuality shows heterosexuals that, on the one hand, gay people face comments and exclusions in ways straight people do not. On the other hand, reversing such questions also indicates to heterosexuals that thinking about their sexuality and its relationship to social customs and institutions would be a good idea.

Pedagogies are meant to be challenging so these queer traditions engage the difficulties of learning head on. Any form of teaching requires both meeting students where they are, in all their contradictory and complex positionings, and also negotiating together toward new understandings, stimulating and responding to curiosity, and encouraging questioning. Change of any kind can simultaneously be joyous and nearly impossible; students may already have changed attitudes, identities, and communities well beyond what teachers expect or understand. Maintaining the difficulties of challenging what many take to be the necessary starting point of "normal," while also disrupting normalcy, entails risk taking and struggle and the realization that simple solutions are complex and even intentionally complex solutions re-create deceptive simplicities (Britzman, 1995; Britzman & Gilbert, 2004; Bryson & de Castell, 1993). So the larger point in this chapter is to examine how such disruptions and criticality will inevitably drift back to certainties and comforts of normalcy while trying to move toward new understandings of difference, whether related to LGBTQ issues or other categories.

The larger frame of the difficulty of LGBTQ pedagogy recognizes that school professionals also face practical challenges about which they need to think in complicated ways and also help create better learning relationships. These issues are difficult and raise dilemmas about how to think about LGBTQ youth who are both in need of recognition and want to have some sense of being public, but also want to maintain privacy as well. Teacher educators are not always prepared to understand LGBTQ issues or may resist lessons about homophobia or sexual and gender minority issues when they are part of preservice teacher education (DePalma & Atkinson, 2006; Ferfolja & Robinson, 2004). Nora Hyland (2010) discusses the variety of resistances, including religious objections to homosexuality and a decision to draw the line at LGBTQ issues, even among students who are committed to linking social justice and education. She further shows the unwillingness among some students to see the potential for intersections of race and homosexuality and so to see anti-homophobia lessons as connected to teaching against racism. By using journals as part of her teaching strategy, Hyland found that LGBTQ people of color in her class felt unable to come out, not wanting to risk splitting their allegiance to anti-racism, a position they shared with some of the vocally anti-gay students. The preservice teacher educators with whom Hyland worked found that their own lack of consistency in advocating for social justice while not supporting LGBTQ students was a problem for some of them; and that realization troubled not only the class's sense of community, it caused them to seriously question their self-designation as a social justice advocate and teacher. That they were able to understand these conflicts and to have space prior to entering the teaching profession is at least a positive step. Such difficulties in learning about LGBTQ issues, though, point to the need to have preservice teacher education classes more comprehensively address them, and to provide preservice teachers with more opportunities to reflect and sort out their conflicts before becoming teachers. But conflicts and shortcomings persist and so the challenge for educators and students alike is to be watchful for how our teaching and learning is bound up in persistent resistances, fears, and difficulties, as well as curiosities.

For all this queer complexity, there are also practical, day-to-day issues that need to be attended to as well. Professional development workshops on LGBTQ issues raise topics teachers and administrators are concerned with, including the complexity of what "being out" means for students. Recognizing that students have diverse forms of identity and recognition related to their contexts for being out can lead school professionals to be cautious about whether they will inadvertently out students to their families, whether students who are out in particular school contexts are out in other contexts as well, and to also think about the limitations of the meaning of being out. Students may be out to one another but not to parents, out in community centers but not in schools, and so on. So the simple discourse of "out" as a once and for all decision, with clear meaning, is inaccurate (Loutzenheiser & MacIntosh, 2004; Rasmussen, 2004; Talburt, 2004). There are, of course, more students who are LGBTQ in any school than those who are known or recognized as such and more students who are affected by bias or curious about sexuality and gender identity. School professionals also wonder about what terms they should use when discussing LGBTQ-related topics, and how to more accurately work with students whose self-identifications are more complex than they may be used to, perhaps well aware that youth are pushing beyond the gender binary and developing their own terms and meanings for sexuality and gender identity. Teachers and school leaders may also be concerned that discussing LGBTQ issues will either open space for homophobic comments or make other students uncomfortable. Students who are transgender show schools how much seemingly mundane issues are framed by gender normativity: using restrooms, changing for gym, being called by a gender-related first name they choose, choosing which table to sit at in the lunchroom, which subjects to excel at, or which games to play at recess. Thinking about the possible presence of LGBTQ families means being careful to not assume all families have a mother and father. Clearly this is not only an issue for LGBTQ families but for other diverse family forms. But keeping in mind such diversities, ensuring that representations throughout the curricula do so too, and that meeting with diverse families is something expected rather than something startling, all go a long way toward ensuring all students and all families are invited into the school community. Some inclusion of diversity may seem relatively easy to accomplish, but each addition can also act as a reminder that "normal" assumptions about families, young people, gender, and sexual orientation are always lurking behind attempts to make schools more welcoming. It is easy to fall back into normal and too easy for normal to become exclusionary.

Even intentions to make safe spaces in schools can be problematic. Simple strategies to make schools safe may implicitly avoid education that considers the pleasurable riskiness of sexuality, the difficulties of differences in identities, and even the playful exchanges that work at the edges of normal (Mayo, 2011; Stengel & Weems, 2010). Balancing forms of education that acknowledge difficulty and difference while also maintaining physical safety can be challenging. Changing how to act and teach in the context of difference is difficult. Weems (2010) suggests that such shifts in classroom practice require new metaphors, trading the relationship between schooling and comfort for the archness of queer camp, the use of doubled meaning and defensive or even offensive humor to disrupt norms. Weems enacts her own camp reading by redefining what camp can mean, emphasizing diverse globalized meanings by considering pushing the meaning of the word "camp" out of localized slang, attitude, and practice and into global migration and movement. She pushes us to think instead about camp as global relocation, in the sense of refugee camps, and to be aware that every home-like gesture is made in the context of difference. This shift defamiliarizes pedagogy from its too easy assumption of direction and meaning, and opens students to forms of knowing that come from queer and transnational cultures (Weems, 2010). For Barbara Stengel (2010), addressing the difficulties of education means taking fear more seriously and understanding how the call for safety may be the occasion that raises fearfulness. Indeed, some approaches to educating for safety maintain the distances between students. Because attempts at school safety may position LGBTQ youth as only at risk or only innocent victims, such discourses and pedagogical approaches limit how sexuality and gender identity are understood in school communities and also limit how LGBTQ youth appear to their peers and school professionals (Hackford-Peer, 2010). Shifting away from pedagogies that seek only to protect students from difficult forms of understanding requires taking on new kinds of curiosities and being aware of the sorts of ignorances that have structured schools' relation to reproducing "normal" unquestioningly.

SEX AND NON-SEX

Addressing LGBTQ issues means confronting both the oversexualization and undersexualization of LGBTQ people—and anyone else, for that matter. Schools may be reluctant to teach about diverse sexualities, even within the context of teaching about diverse families, fearful that raising the idea of LGBTQ families means discussing sex. Families are and always have been complicated and diverse: single parent–headed households, blended families, adoptive families, extended families, grandparent-headed households, and foster families all also potentially raise questions. Even very young students understand that love and attraction are part of what brings families together, and they know the relationship between families and reproduction, if not the fullest understanding of sex that they will have later. But it is also the case that we often have a very mistaken view of what young people know and don't know about sex, sexuality, relationships, and families. They know these issues from their own experience, what they see in the media, and the stories they read. Sexuality may seem to haunt LGBTQ issues in particular, but sexuality is a part of many other school-based topics as well, in ways sometimes not acknowledged. School personnel, historical and fictional figures, and a wide variety of school practices and events assume that people will be romantically interested in one another, date, partner, and marry. In such mundane examples, even if sexuality is part of relationships, clearly relationships are more than sex: They involve emotions, responsibilities, identities, and communities. Thinking about relational ethics in ways that include gender identity and sexual orientation can include the history and present experience of LGBTQ community, coming out, rethinking gender, rethinking sexuality, how to negotiate different contexts of acceptance, or how to learn from LGBTQ adults in a climate structured by fear of pedophilia.

Transyouth, too, experience oversexualization when they try to use restrooms appropriate to their chosen gender or when their complex gender isn't seen to fit with either gendered space. Responses to gender nonconforming or gender transitioning or students who have transitioned to their chosen gender indicate schools' fear that "cross-gender" contact indicates something threatening. In such situations they both misrecognize the gender identity of the transgender student and import the threat of sex, perhaps to anchor the more unfamiliar discomfort related to transgender issues. For students who are transitioning from male to female, school professionals may prioritize concern about sexual harassment whether or not anyone has indicated discomfort and sometimes restrict youth to using staff restrooms based on the assumption that gender nonconforming students are in and of themselves frightening.

Undersexualization of LGBTQ issues is a problem as well, stressing only bias issues and not recognizing or educating about the particular needs of LGBTQ youth in sex education. It is hard to understand how so many school districts decided to avoid addressing HIV/AIDS even when it was a leading cause of adolescent death (Mayo, 2004a), and yet such exclusions continue even today. Heterosexually active students, too, often do not get the answers they need from curricula or teachers. In her study of debates over sex education in a variety of different U.S. states, Nancy Kendall (2013) found that no matter what the official approach to sex education was, classes were more educationally effective if they engaged critical analysis of the meanings of sexuality and opened space for young people to learn more about issues they were curious about or urgently felt the need to know. This kind of critical analysis, Kendall argues, is key to developing a robust democracy and ensuring that sexuality is more clearly linked to political and community-related issues. Her point is that sex education ought to be a space for thinking about civic engagement, enabling young people to analyze the limitations of their sexuality education, the ways they want to be learning, and the kinds of responsibilities they have to their various communities. Such arguments have long been made from LGBTQ adult communities—that schools are underpreparing LGBTQ youth for their eventual participation in such communities by not recognizing the need for them to take responsibility for their sexual health.

Teaching toward a critical analysis of sexuality in schools can help students to analyze how cultural and political issues related to sexuality and youth are interlinked. Having school personnel think about this same question might also raise the problematic assumption that young people's sexuality or gender identity ought not to be taken seriously because they are too young to know who they are. The objection that youth are not sufficiently mature to know their identity, though, does not mean that they ought not to be able to learn more about diverse identities or that they ought not be protected from bias against sexual or gender minority–related bias.

These specific issues are also related to broader questions: How do schools deal with contentious issues in general? Do schools shut down anti-LGBTQ harassment, but never actually address LGBTQ issues in curricula or provide any positive indication of LGBTQ relationships and communities? Do schools have spaces for LGBTQ students to socialize and organize with one another? Can schools provide support to teachers to enable them to incorporate more curricular representations and pedagogies related to LGBTQ issues? Are educators who want to provide LGBTQ and other students with lessons or extracurricular activities able to find support in their schools to do so? Trying to face the difficulties of these issues and maintaining a sense of their difficulty while so doing is at least a better start than shutting down education through prohibition.

CRITICAL QUEER THINKING AND QUEER DISCIPLINES

In many ways LGBTQ issues have made their way into classrooms in the questions and identities students already bring in and the prominence of LGBTQ issues in current events. Thinking about what teaching and educating involves further raises some issues that are linked to the sense of *queer* that means seeing at an angle or bending norms. Critical thinking, for instance, asks us to queer our commonplace understanding of concepts by which we know anything and to instead stop and think from a new perspective. As we encourage students to engage in such discussions of key categories, lessons provide them with strategies for countering restrictive norms and help them develop their critical insights into their own sense of identity and communities, and grappling with how to denormalize their sense of themselves and others. In many ways, then, as educators we are already working on the project of intentionally queering classrooms. As we think about adding information and critical engagement activities to history, social studies, literature, and art lessons, ensuring that information about LGBTQ people, communities, and movements in history is included is one way to begin to change the dominant viewpoint on analysis of issues, a way to challenge the school-based practices of reinforcing gender norms. Adding curricular materials or suggesting analytic approaches that take sexual orientation and gender identity into account more centrally may reinforce how distinct LGBTQ communities and identities are, but these additive approaches, while helpful in some ways, by easily including information, do not yet queer the issues. Teaching gender normative students about the process of learning and enacting gender shows that all students understand what nonconformity means and that all students, too, have probably experienced someone pressuring them to act correctly for their gender. Cisgender girls, for instance, understand the pressures to dress like a lady, defer to male attention, and know too, that turning down male attention may result in their being called homophobic terms. Cisgendered boys know that if they show weakness they will be corrected by either being called girls, homophobic epithets, or by being told to "walk it off." The distinctiveness of LGBTQ-related bias, in other words, may not be so distinct in the particular experience of it, but like sexual harassment, ubiquitous for boys and girls, the negative effects are much stronger for those in the nondominant position. For normatively gendered youth, teasing or pressure to act correctly may almost be ignored since it does not usually interrupt their intentional acts of identity. For girls, the experience of sexual harassment reminds them that the dominant meaning of their gender, however much our policies and norms are intent on changing it, is to be objectified. So thinking about LGBTQ experiences as shared among all students may help us see how pressures to be normal affect all genders, and at the same time many students who experience these pressures will nonetheless accrue more social privilege from their identities as gender normative and heterosexual.

That LGBTQ identities simply exist, of course, is often enough to make students who have seemingly had a life organized around dominant identities and dominant sexualities have some anxiety. And as a turn to queer pedagogy insists on examining the complications that race, class, gender, and ethnicity bring to what is defined as either LGBTQ or other terms that resonate more with members of other cultures, such pedagogies need to both insist on queer presence and being careful that one version of queer does not itself become another form of normal—*normal* meaning White, male, privileged, exclusively attracted to men, and so on. In other words, those who teach and learn about LGBTQ subjects are also constantly running up against the potential return of comfortable categories to dissident identities and communities in ways that minimize their dissidence and critique of norms. That turn to comfort or the recoil from discomfort is a feature of how learning takes place, so educators should not be surprised if, for instance, during a film in which there are LGBTQ speakers or during a lesson on a novel in which the sexualities characters have are not definitively heterosexual, students may tend to titter, shift in their seats, or occasionally break out into hysterical laughter. Students for whom such representations may be particularly important may act in those ways too, using expressions of homophobia to hide their own identities more firmly (Clark & Blackburn, 2009). Those times are likely fading since so many LGBT and queer images are now in the mass media, but even shifting popular culture into the seemingly rarefied context of academia can generate either discomfort or ecstasy, and when we work to disrupt our own comfort with what counts as queer, we also put ourselves into that same position our students are in: working through, around, with our discomforts about the limits of what we, even with all our careful thinking and living, think is normal.

Lessons that queer a school community or push students to understand exclusions can occur even in subject areas that might seem unlikely. Kat Rands (2013) explains how a subject like mathematics, seemingly disconnected from social issues, can be used to help teach middle school students about transgender-related bias and intervention. Like others in critical and social justice math (Gutiérrez, 2002; Gutstein, 2003), Rands argues that math has to be understood within a social context and that doing so not only increases students' understanding of math by applying it to an example relevant to their and their peers' school experience, it also entails teaching more than math. Rands uses the example of proportional thinking and statistics-related processes, all of which are part of middle school math standards. Because proportions and ratios require understanding how to *unitize*, that is, make things part of a group, and how to *partition*, that is, distinguish concepts and things from one another, such discussions can readily be applied to the kinds of social divisions students encounter in schools. Extending this discussion of concepts to mathematics work, Rands suggests using the GLSEN reports to learn about statistics and do their own studies on how often their peers have intervened in harassment. Teachers can then explain that smaller studies help us see the specifics of a situation as it is experienced in detail but larger studies can provide a fuller picture of many people's experiences, helping show trends. Further, Rands (2013) wants such projects to lead to action in schools, helping students see how transphobia affects all students and how important it is for bystanders to find ways to intervene in gender- and gender identity–related bias.

Librarians can provide another kind of curricular support by providing students interested in LGBTQ issues with a fuller array of resources. Ensuring that school libraries have representation of LGBTQ children's or young adult fiction can provide youth with a way to think through these diversities on their own time. By providing a broad array of LGBTQ resources, libraries also enable friends or family members of LGBTQ people or students curious about LGBTQ issues with a place to read and think further (Flecker & Gutteridge, 2008). Fiction that suggests diverse family forms or personal identities, without specifically naming sexual orientation or gender identity, also helps complicate the constant representation of only normative heterosexuality, families, and identities (Jenkins, 1993). Thinking more critically about reading practices, including how readers identify with characters different from them and analyzing how narrative encourages or discourages such identifications, may enable or reinforce in students the ability to read themselves into texts in which they are not represented: Reading mobilizes identifications and desires with and beyond the text (Britzman & Gilbert, 2004). Readers, in other words, not only work within the conventions of reading, they push against meaning, fill in their desires as they read, and complicate texts beyond what may be taught about them.

Heather Sykes (2004) provides a complex account of why teachers in physical education may not intervene in the sexist or heterosexist bias in sports, complicating the context for anti-bias education in schools by focusing on teacher identity and motivations. Her analysis separates out teachers who stop harassment through a desire to police, that is, simply stop the harassment, those who want students to think about the injuries they are affecting with biased language, and those who take on the injuries of the speech themselves in what she sees as a masochistic turning back of student hostility onto themselves. Such an analysis highlights the kinds of risks and working through bias that teachers, especially those who are related to the forms of bias in which they are intervening, undertake.

Taking education about sexual orientation and gender identity out of the context of particular subjects entirely, Eric Rofes (2005) encourages teachers to themselves think and act with a more complex understanding of how their teaching is embodied and how their embodiment has social and political meaning. He pushes teachers to consider how their gender presentation is part of their pedagogy, how they shift ways of communicating to use what they know about gender, and how their presentation of a gendered self is meant to indicate, as well, their sexual orientation. Like other work on gender and female teacher style (Atkinson, 2008), Rofes (2005) describes the dilemma of wanting to have parts of his gay identity mesh with his teaching. But he is also aware that his bodily presentation, his gender performance, and other cultural meanings associated with gayness are understood in ways that stimulate cultural anxieties. His very presentation of self, in all its varied intentional and unintentional uses of gender and sexual identity, is part of his pedagogy, in ways that help his students understand subject material and in ways that help his students understand him as a teacher with a complex sexuality and gender. His point is that he, as a gay teacher, has to take these complexities into account and also that he is sensitive to the suggestion, when he neglects to take gender into account in his style of teaching, that he needs to think more critically about it. In other words, like Capper's (1999) observation that gay and lesbian educational administrative students are more willing to take other forms of diversity seriously as central to their practice, Rofes's pedagogy shows both his attention to his gender, as far as he himself recognizes it, and his willingness to listen carefully to what colleagues say about how he uses various forms of gender, like fem or butch (gay cultural formations that tap into kinds of femininity and masculinity, respectively), in his teaching and to make those decisions part of his intentional critical reflection.

Rofes's work and that of other theorists (Bryson & de Castell, 1993; Britzman, 1995) focus on the educational aspects of queerness, linking it to innovation, subversion, and even unrecognizable forms of transgression. The new forms of identity emerging out of such intentional recodings of gender identity and sexuality may be harder to see immediately, given our usual attachment to understanding through the lens of normalcy, and so more queer identities have to be discerned or decoded, or left in the realm of being unrecognizable. A queer pedagogy or a pedagogy aimed at teaching queerly would build on the kinds of oppositional readings that LGBTQ people and other minorities have always been very good at doing, finding the hints of nondominant people in stories where they aren't represented, speculating about the possibilities of attractions among literary figures where they aren't exactly explicitly spelled out but nonetheless structure the story (Sedgwick, 1990). In her work with Latina/o LGBTQ students, Tanya Diaz-Kozlowski (2013) found the students eager to connect with her on the basis of their shared Latina/o identity and enthusiastically explaining their lives and challenges. Diaz-Kozlowski's willingness to respond to their intensities and to provide Latina/o LGBTQ youth with an adult educator/mentor who could understand the intersections of their ethnic, linguistic, and familial background shows both how rare such connections may be for some students but how energetically they respond to an educator willing to share.

Intense speculation, critical interest, and at times perverse, reading-against-the grain curiosity are part of the queer relationship between LGBTQ people and learning and indeed of the queerness of education in general. In schools, many students may view class participation as "so gay." It is hard to be nonconforming and passionately involved in the exchange of ideas. In this sort of potentially intellectually alienating setting, the desire to learn is itself queer, remarkable, and exuberant. The queerness of wanting to learn matches up well with the queerness of wanting to teach. For both the queer learner and queer teacher, categories that are by no means mutually exclusive, education is a scene of excess, speculation, and passion. It isn't always considered normal to have passion for one's studies so the queer scene of education, where classes, even if initially in the pose of disinterest, do come to enjoy the intimacy of intellectual connection and the intensity of learning, debate, and classroom discussion show in their enthusiasms a kind of disruption of norms.

RELIGIOUS TENSIONS

Two interlinked issues are particularly challenging to education: religion and pleasure, especially the pleasure of speculation, that is, thinking about sexuality and the pleasures of community. Despite the large numbers of organized religions that respect and support LGBTQ people, there is still a divide in terms of respectability between religious thought and sexual and gender minorities. Even in schools willing to represent LGBTQ students, parents, and topics, concern about offending religious traditions or causing controversies may dampen educational plans or impede student organizations like GSAs. Schools may overcorrect and put limitations on LGBTQ lessons or clubs for fear of the responses from religious organizations. Differences in laws and policies across the United States also means that teachers in some states may find that providing support for LGBTQ students and allies is more challenging than it might be in other areas.

These are complicated times to be a teacher. Even as the Supreme Court has overturned the Section 3 of the Defense of Marriage Act and enabled the appeals court ruling in California to overturn Proposition 8, opening California as a same-sex marriage state, many other states have made same-sex marriage illegal. As for education, students in different states have considerably different access to learning about sexual orientation and gender identity. To do what teachers need to do and respect all the students, classrooms need to include people whose backgrounds or whose identities may seem to put them at odds with one another. Being a teacher, for that matter, puts professionals potentially at odds with parts of their own upbringing and identities, and attempts to work through these issues in preservice teacher education highlight the distance between education students' hopes for their commitment to social justice and the limitations, often religiously based, some find when confronting homophobia (Hyland, 2010). In such situations, it may be helpful to consider some similarities between religion and sexuality. There are some parallels between the processes of coming to have a faith, as in confirmation, conversion, or some other mature indication of belonging, and the process of critically assessing sexual or gender identity, as in coming out. Or, if one views religion as a matter of family tradition and sexuality as something one is born with, there are also similarities. Each, in other words, is a complex identity, each generally involves a relationship to a community, and each group, depending on the religion and/or sexuality, may have a sense of fragility about its place in public school. Christians may feel embattled by a secular classroom, people of faith who are not Christian, but instead believe in Judaism or Islam or Buddhism or any one of a number of other faiths, may feel excluded by the pervasive influence of Christianity on many policies, days off, and casual references. Youth who are not religious at all may feel that the assumption is that everyone has a religion and there is no room for them to express their commitment to humanism or atheism. Schools, then, when addressing religion may not realize the extent to which they are immersed in dominant religious culture and they may not be inclined, either, to interrupt what they take as normal.

Teaching about religions and sexualities can also open discussion of the fact there are religions that are respectful of sexual diversity and others that define themselves against it. In other words, take the opportunity of these discussions to point out differences within and between religions, not to challenge anyone's faith but to complicate what religion means in a given social context. Such pedagogical approaches can explore the longer history of why certain religions decided to use prohibition against sodomy to define themselves. Religious historian Mark D. Jordan (1998), for instance, explains that Christian theologians began to separate out sodomy for special comment because those theologians were also engaged in teaching prohibitions on nonprocreative heterosexual sex or any sex that involved pleasure. According to Jordan, the move to do this began in medieval theology to single out an act that is sexual, pleasurable, and nonprocreative, regardless of whatever gender engages in it. Pleasure, then, not the particular activities that same-sex couples—or different-sex couples—engage in, was the key problem for these theologians, not sexual orientation itself. The ensuing use of sodomy as a shorthand for those prohibitions and the eventual singling out of gay people for the sin of sodomy came much later (Jordan, 1998).

Even an examination of the contemporary claims that the United States should maintain a Biblical definition of marriage can open a discussion of the diversity of marriage in the early years of many faiths. A close look through the Bible, for instance, shows a wide diversity of marriages, including marriages with concubines, multiple wives, close relatives, and combinations thereof. Other histories of how same-sex couples came to be the main target of conservative Christianity might trace how particular segments of faith groups substituted gay issues for their earlier anger at racial integration. Whether racial desegregation or same-sex marriage, some people hold closely to their traditional view of how society should be organized, and however much I or anyone else might want to see it otherwise, this is a difficult argument to make in terms that such religious commitments might understand.

But however much schools need to respect religious difference and provide extracurricular opportunities for religious students to organize, schools are not religious institutions. They are central institutions for preparing future citizens for diverse democracy. So the responsibilities of educators are different from other forms of responsibility or commitment that people working in schools might have in other areas of their lives. These commitments to education, service, and faith are not so easily untangled for many people, of course, and that may be precisely why educators need to have professional standards. Those standards, different in each state, vary in their embrace of respect for sexual and gender diversity. At the same time, it is crucial that schools not derogate religious faith but instead find ways to maintain respectful relationships between all students, school personnel, and community members. Further, while a robust sense of what democracy means could help provide an educational context where LGBTQ issues become part of what it means to be educated, obstacles remain. Even when teachers, administrators, or counselors enter schools supportive of LGBTQ issues they may find their institutional position and organization makes such support difficult. As Barrie Thorne (1993) details so well, schools are both sorting mechanisms for gender, separating girls and boys for little apparent reason, and also a context for varied salience of gender and gender border crossings. McCready (2010) shows the limitations of school programs for encouraging space for intersectional identities, noting that racism in Gay-Straight Alliances, for instance, keeps LGBTQ youth of color from joining. While each researcher also notes openings where young people work against norms and remake identities or change their schools, nonetheless, the heteronormativity of educational institutions may seem intransigent (Bryson & de Castell, 1993).

TEACHING AND LEARNING FOR ETHICAL RELATIONS

C. J. Pascoe (2007) examined the use of expressions of homophobia to help young men bond together in high school. By playing with and joking about the potential for attraction, young men negotiate masculinity through sexism and homophobia, but also sometimes create playful and pleasurable scenes of gender nonconformity. Many of these negotiations are meant to reinstall sexual and gendered norms, but some of them slide into the giddiness of trying new ways of doing gender and sexuality, even for a moment or even in jest, as in performing same-sex attraction in skits, both mocking it and showing the pleasures and even perversity of such flirtations, too. Other sorts of pleasures related to gender and sexual orientation worry teachers, staff, and administrators, but clearly get the attention of young people thinking about their present and their futures. Sexuality is usually relational and so meeting with people who are thinking about diverse sexuality or rethinking and reinhabiting gender in new ways may be something best done in a supportive atmosphere of diverse peers. It is hard for young teachers to maintain their support of all students if they enter schools where institutional support is evidently lacking. Further, it may be easier to support identities that we as adults understand than to make room for the new formations that young people create through their desires for their own bodies, social positions, relationships, and communities. It is difficult, too, for teachers to allow young people space to try out new identities and not step in when young people seem to be engaging in activities that are ecstatic but do not necessarily appear to be productive or recognizable. But if changes to gender and sexuality–based norms are to be part of education, it is important for adults to ensure that classrooms can be open spaces of productive play (and still be watchful for forms of play that verge into bias and harassment).

Sexualities and genders of all varieties need to be attentive to creating ethical relationships, thinking not only about how one is situated in those relations, that is, thinking carefully about sexual orientation and gender identity but thinking also about the obligations and joys of creating communities and partnerships based on desire and care. Being open to new formations of identity related to gender and sexuality is part of how such ethical relationships are developed. Recognizing that each of us has an insufficient ability to understand one another's complexity but that we need to try to do so can help to remind all of us that we both want recognition of our particularities and that we also know we exceed the ability of anyone, including ourselves, to fully know and understand who we are and what our motivations and desires are.

While this book has covered various historical trajectories of sexual orientation and gender identity, there are still other possibilities for opening the subject of sexuality and gender that will be developed. Education is a process that moves learners of all generations from where they start to where they will go next, all the while being more contradictory and uncertain than that progress seems to indicate. As difficult and challenging as pedagogies that address sexuality and gender identity are, ignoring them is a bad option. A few districts have tried to avoid all these discussions, and states have considered passing educational laws characterized as "don't say gay" bills requiring teachers to have nothing to say about gay issues. In such situations, like Anoka-Hennepin, anti-gay students filled the power vacuum left when teachers were no longer able to intervene, rates of bullying rose, and multiple suicides occurred. Deciding to "not" educate is an inadequate solution.

Instead, I suggest educating tentatively, carefully, and with an understanding that education related to LGBTQ and intersectional issues requires organizational support and bringing in diverse colleagues. These are not issues that can be addressed without cooperation with other school professionals who can support anti-homophobic commitments even when institutional pressures seem to suggest such issues should be ignored. Educate tentatively, because the categories by which educators understand historical and contemporary people may only be vaguely accurate and are in the process of being remade through social change and generational innovation. We claim as "gay" historical figures who didn't live in a social context that would have allowed them to understand what it's like to be who we are living in a time that seems to have more possibilities for LGBTQ people to organize communities and relationships. On the other hand, we are now living in a context where over thirty states have made a constitutional amendment against same-sex marriage so LGBTQ people do understand what it is like for some aspects of our lives to be illegal. For people who are gender nonconforming, knowing that police could have stopped them for not wearing enough items of gender appropriate clothing just a few decades ago or knowing that their style of dress might have rendered their choice of occupation impossible at a different historical juncture may reinforce a sense of long-standing exclusion. On the other hand, learning about subcultures of sometimes cross-dressing lesbians in higher education or the public culture of gender nonconforming fairies, who sometimes considered themselves a third sex in turn of the century New York, might provide a sense of connection across time. Learning, too, about the politics, art, and communities that LGBTQ people have made, whether a century ago, during the AIDS crisis, or now, will all add to how LGBTQ youth see themselves and how they are seen by other students.

Educating carefully entails thinking about what LGBTQ and ally students need and want and thinking about how to avoid having adult definitions, resistances, and restrictions frame all the lessons. Schools may be intentionally restrictive places; even educators who want to help LGBTQ and ally youth are so used to the structures of norms that they are not able to see how they are impeding youth who are trying to create new identities and relationships. Part of the process of educating carefully means recognizing that youth are already opening spaces, not all of them school-based, and working with and through the changing definitions of gender and sexuality around them. Schools may, in many cases, be coming to these dynamics late or perhaps inevitably creating barriers to such changes. Providing young people with opportunities to hone their critical capacity, their research skills, and their abilities to challenge their own biases are part of what schools can do to ensure that the next generations will be careful to not replicate the exclusions of earlier generations.

Understanding that advocating for LGBTQ and other minority students entails creating supportive connections with others may help educators plan more effectively for school, curricular, and pedagogical change. When I meet with novice teachers, they often say that they went into education determined to be advocates for all students but that they found the institutional setting of schools worked against their hope to do so. With heteronormativity embedded in simple graphics that circulate about dances, obvious heteronormativity even in abstinence-only education, and the seeming obliviousness with which teachers and administrators allow anti-LGBTQ discourses to pervade school spaces, they feel that schools work purposefully to stifle their attempts to change those spaces and practices.

It is crucial, then, that teachers, administrators, and school staff who want to make changes make those changes in relationship with others. These are not things easily done alone, and planning for the inevitable failures to interrupt larger institutional practices as well as microaggressions can help us understand the sociability of politics, as much as the sociability of sexuality. Making spaces for LGBTQ youth to do more with that space than we imagine is a major challenge for those of us whose histories were shaped in directions we might not yet understand and whose future is also as yet unclear. As educators aimed toward new futures, too, we need to understand that we may even create problems. Even when we can think more carefully about LGBTQ issues and other intersecting minority concerns as well, we will nonetheless doubtless make mistakes. Our openings will be of the wrong sorts, the space we organize will be insufficient or even restrictive. By putting adult formations at the center of helping youth think educatively and act ethically about their sexualities and gender, we may overlook the fact that the young people already do have lives, of course, and the ability to take the spaces they want, at least to some extent. But our efforts at least make clear that we understand LGBTQ and ally students are present and that schools as institutions reflect democratic and diverse possibility. My work with queer youth and ally organizations has helped me see the creation of associational identities, increasingly interested in situating their discussion and action in relation to one another. I don't think these are simple utopian gestures, and I recognize that young organizations cannot undo the

institutional and historical situation of segregated schools, and that neighbor-
hoods and friendship networks, too, continue patterns of racial, class-based,
and gender segregation. Nevertheless, with more concerted effort at interrupting historical exclusions, youth alliances can be exuberant sites for exploring
difference and relationality. And helping youth trace out their roots in a vast
network of similar social projects, however tenuously connected to where they
will take us, also provides, if not guidance, a sense of simultaneous continuity
and discontinuity, a contradictory gesture but one as close to a definition of
education as anything else.

CHAPTER 5

Supporting Student Extracurricular and Creative Efforts to Educate Schools on LGBTQ Issues

Despite many of the obstacles and challenges we detail in other chapters, LGBT students and allies have made significant progress in improving school communities. This chapter examines the growth of extracurricular and curricular activities organized by students and supportive faculty, especially the increasing numbers of Gay-Straight Alliances (GSAs). Drawing on student accounts of what GSAs have done to help their experiences in school, we examine the role of GSAs in helping students organize against multiple forms of bias, draw in diverse members, and provide publicity to issues often not covered in official curricula. I also draw on information from recent studies to show the role of GSAs in helping even students who are not members feel supported in schools and potentially decrease the number of LGBTQ dropouts. This chapter examines other forms of LGBTQ-related student activism, like the Day of Silence, that also engage learning about sexualities and rights-related issues, as well as projects that help schools address LGBTQ issues.

GAY-STRAIGHT ALLIANCES AND ASSOCIATIONS ACROSS DIFFERENCE

Gay-Straight Alliances bring together students from diverse sexual orientations and gender identities. Organizations like GSAs and other activities described in this chapter show that students have significant impact on the school community, and also that students who are different from one another can and do work together in many schools. Their ability to form these groups has been challenged in many different locations but the most frequent way they can justify their place in schools is by using the Equal Access Act (EAA) of 1984. Understanding the history and the applications of the EAA can provide educators with a firmer grounding in both the debates around its use and its purposes, and hopefully find strategies, as well, for helping young people continue to work to improve their school communities. The kinds of associations encouraged by GSAs and other coalition groups can help encourage students to be curious about difference and help them learn, as well, how to organize to make that curiosity and respect a fuller part of school culture. Such groups, though, need to be encouraged to work beyond the exclusions that they may act out, whether racism, sexism, transphobia, or other biases.

Students involved in GSAs are often all, regardless of their sexual orientation or gender identity, involved in rethinking norms around gender and sexuality and involved, as well, in interrogating how bias shapes the lives of gender and sexual minorities. In the best tradition of education, too, they take their curiosity about others and push themselves to move into learning and socializing across identity boundaries. Because their questioning, curiosity, and social activities are both personal and political, these groups are notable for reminding us that all identities are socially formed and negotiated, and further, that learning to be any sort of sexual or gender identity requires supportive and challenging engagement with others. I have argued elsewhere that this process is deeply ethical (Mayo, 2004a, 2004b) and while there are complications to the kinds of community created by GSAs—exclusions based on race, gender, or trans identity, for instance—many of the young people with whom I have worked and researched have shown respectful interest in one another's differences, too.

GSAs are not perfect, though, and often parallel the segregation patterns around them. Schools remain racially, ethnically, and socioeconomically segregated institutions, and friendship networks, even in racially diverse schools, continue to be segregated as well (Ryabov, 2011). While diverse schools have a higher percentage of cross-racial friendships, the larger the number of minorities (Quillian & Campbell, 2001), it is also true that the more racial diversity there is in a school, the more likely students will form friendships with other students of the same race or ethnicity (Ryabov, 2011). Residential discrimination has only a weak effect on school-based choices though it does remain part of the explanation for racial segregation in friendship (Mouw & Entwisle, 2006). Friendships are also potentially disrupted by differences in sexual orientation (Poteat, Espelage, & Koenig, 2009). The disproportionate number of young women involved in GSAs, in addition, has caused comment (Perrotti & Westheimer, 2001), though whether all the girls usually identified as heterosexual actually self-identify that way is a more complex issue (Mayo, 2007). In addition, differential experiences and outcomes from gender-based harassment may mean that young people are less understanding about gender differences. Gender segregation in friendship networks continues through adolescence, in part because young women find other young women more sympathetic conversational partners (Mehta & Strough, 2010). Gray (2007) and Blackburn (2005) each describe LGBT and queer youth organizing and socializing with one another, often in public and in ways not legible to those around them, developing networks for socializing and support in plain sight that counter the exclusions they experience in schools. Another study on a small sample indicates that LGB youth friendship networks segregate based on sexual orientation because of structural constraints and heteronormativity (Ueno, Wright, Gayman, & McCabe, 2012). GSAs provide not only an indication that the general school environment recognizes the challenges of heteronormativity and homophobia, they also encourage students of different sexual orientations and gender identities to meet and socialize.

The benefits of this ability to organize across differences accrues to all genders and sexualities, including heterosexual students (Lee, 2002). Students who are not out in school but are either questioning their sexuality or have decided they are LGBTQ but don't want it known in school may be less likely to support a GSA, even if it's something they would have done when they thought they were straight:

> Before I came out I was different. I would always be there for everything. I was pro diversity everywhere. You want me to march for lesbians? I'll march for lesbians. I didn't mind being called gay. It didn't affect me. When it turned out it did apply to me, I'm not gonna be there. (quoted in Mayo, 2004a, p. 154)

Her shift in comfort marks her realization that the level of safety she felt in her school was perhaps a bit exaggerated. Toomey, McGuire, and Russell (2012) found that heterosexual peers rated their schools safer than LGB students did, and further, that LGB students rated their schools safer from gender identity harassment than transgender students did. Gay-Straight Alliances may provide students with opportunities for closer conversations with sexual and gender minority students to help them understand the problems, even if they are heterosexual and do not experience homophobia or transphobia as unsafe.

For other heterosexually identified students, the Gay-Straight Alliance represents a space where they feel more comfortable, whether they more closely identify with LGBTQ students (Ruenzel, 1999) or because they are in some way also different from the majority of students in their schools. Sometimes allies initially feel uncomfortable, caught in a bind wanting to be supportive but not wanting to be known as gay, but also not wanting to publicly disavow LGBTQ identities:

> People assume I'm LGBT identified. When I tell them I'm not, first they doubt me, and then they wonder why I would get involved. At school I no longer have an identity separate from the GSA, it's not Nate . . . anymore, it's "Nate of the GSA." (Parrish, 2002)

Ally students point to the challenges of always being known in relation to their advocacy for the rights of LGBTQ students. Heterosexual allies also relate that their experience in GSAs and LGBTQ youth conferences gives them an understanding about what sexual and gender identity minority students feel like in a heterosexist school climate:

> At first I was a little apprehensive, but the LGBTQ students showed me around, taught me how to dance, offered to let me stay at the hostel with them. We became really close friends. All feelings of alienation were quickly replaced by curiosity for those whose lives were so different from my own and yet so similar to my own. (Baker, 2002)

In addition, LGBT students in schools that have GSAs have fewer negative experiences, including lower suicide risk, fewer symptoms of depression, and fewer incidents of substance abuse (Heck, Flentje, & Cochran, 2011).

GAY-STRAIGHT ALLIANCES AND THE EQUAL ACCESS ACT

Located in about four thousand schools nationwide, Gay-Straight Alliances (GSAs) are one way that LGBTQ youth and allies can organize in schools and receive official recognition and status as student organizations. They are able to form even in school communities that deem their topic as controversial because of the First Amendment protections offered students through the Equal Access Act (EAA) of 1984. The EAA was initially proposed to cover students' religious freedom, based on a concern by conservative legislators that court cases were supporting the rights of gay students to have access to school facilities at a time when restrictions were being put on clergy-led religious activities in public schools. The intention of the early version was to ensure that the Supreme Court decision in *Widmar v. Vincent* (1981), which found that a university unconstitutionally prohibited a religious-based student organization from forming and meeting on campus, could also be applied to public schools. As David Buckel (1999) explains in his analysis of the records of discussion over the proposed act, the topic of sexuality and the potential for the act to protect speech on homosexuality was evident in Congressional debate. Members of Congress expressed concern that the new law could potentially protect speech that was either already protected under the First Amendment or would be illegal because homosexuality was illegal. In addition, by making a clear statement in support of freedom of speech, legislators were concerned that schools would be forced to allow speech about illegal activities (homosexual activity was illegal in many states at the time). Debate centered on the distinction between advocacy of rights for gay people and support of illegal activity. One legislator asserted his belief that gay clubs would not be protected by the bill because gay activity "is unlawful." A colleague's question brought him to specify that support for gay rights would only be unlawful if states prohibit homosexual activity. Pushed further, he finally decided that political activity was different from outlawed sexual activity. Debate over the act shifted it away from its original focus on religion and instead revised it to cover all extracurricular activities in schools that already had a limited open forum, that is, allowed extracurricular groups to form.

Nevertheless, the anxieties represented by this legislator's initial inability to understand the distinction between discussing rights related to sexuality and engaging in sexual activity is an early indication of similar concerns by school personnel, school boards, and community members that have continued to impede students who want to form GSAs. In addition, the confusion around whether schools can support student groups who want to discuss sexuality-related rights has also meant that student groups have trouble finding a faculty sponsor, getting approval from administrators, and avoiding opposition from community members who believe the groups are too controversial or too inappropriate for the school setting (even if not meeting during instructional hours).

The first case to use the Equal Access Act to support the formation of a Gay-Straight Alliance was *Colin v. Orange Unified School District* (2000), and in his decision that underscored the right of the GSA to meet at schools with limited open fora, the judge recalled that First Amendment speech, religious, and associational rights of students were protected by the act:

> Due to the First Amendment, Congress passed an "Equal Access Act" when it wanted to permit religious speech on school campuses. It did not pass a "Religious Speech Access Act" or an "Access for All Students except Gay Students Act" because to do so would be unconstitutional. (Judge Carter, quoted in Biegel, 2010, p. 29)

The EAA has also been successfully used to protect the rights of religious students to form student-led organizations and to use school space, either before or after the regular school day. The EAA does stipulate that "employees or agents of the school or government are present at religious meetings only in a nonparticipatory capacity" (EAA, 1984, 4071(c)3), but districts have sometimes been too restrictive of the rights of religious students and assumed that approving such groups would run them afoul of *Lemon v. Kurtzman's* (1971) requirement that schools avoid excessive entanglement with religion. One area where conservative student religious groups and GSAs have found common cause, in fact, is through their use and need to fully understand the EAA in order to ensure they are each able to meet in districts that may be concerned about allowing potentially controversial groups to organize. In a certain sense, then, the experience of similar obstructions to their ability to meet with like-minded students has the potential to create bonds across groups that may not always share common opinions on other key issues. Many religious groups do support LGBTQ rights so their common understanding of the EAA can give them a further shared vocabulary of solidarity, as well as a shared understanding of the breadth of First Amendment protections for all students.

The EAA also allows schools to restrict student speech based on the rules in *Tinker v. Des Moines Independent Community School District* (1969) that protected student freedom of speech but did recognize that schools had an interest in prohibiting activities and speech that would lead to significant disruption of the school. The ruling in *Colin v. Orange Unified School District* (2000) found that rather than disrupting the school, as the district claimed, the GSA was intent on "preventing the disruptions to education that can take place when students are harassed based on sexual orientation" (Judge Carter, quoted in Biegel, 2010, p. 30).

ATTEMPTS TO RESTRICT GAY-STRAIGHT ALLIANCES

In at least two places—Boyd County, Kentucky, and Salt Lake City, Utah—school boards initially banned all extra curricular groups in their respective districts to avoid having a limited open forum and thus sidestep the federal requirement that they recognize all student groups, effectively banning the GSA. In each of those places, however, litigation led to an eventual continuation of the limited open forum in each district and to the recognition of the Gay-Straight Alliances that were forming in those districts. In Salt Lake City, mass protests on the state capitol grounds by a vast array of diverse groups banned from meeting after school—and in support of the GSA's right to meet—helped turn the tide; this action represents the kind of collaboration that can emerge across identity categories and interests when diverse groups of students are faced with the same obstacles. Banned clubs included those organized around Latina/o, African American, Polynesian, Native American, and Asian issues, as well as Students Against Drunk Driving, Young Democrats, and Young Republicans.

The Salt Lake City case, *East High School PRISM Club v. Seidel* (2000), went through a variety of different attempts to prohibit the GSA, including a district decision to allow only clubs that were curriculum-related in order to maintain a closed forum, not a limited open forum. The district application form indicated the standard and asked applicants to show how the after-school club would fit their criteria:

> In order to qualify as a Student Club that is directly related to the curriculum, the club must meet one or more of the following criteria. Check all that apply.

- The subject matter of the club is actually taught or soon will be taught in a regular course offered at the school.
- The subject matter of the club concerns the body of courses as a whole.
- Participation in the club is required for a particular course.
- Participation in the club results in academic credit.

In making their request, the proposed club, People Recognizing Important Social Movements Club (PRISM), indicated that the issues they were covering matched all the criteria and explained they were going to be "engaging in the ongoing dialogue in our community" over such issues as the Boy Scouts' prohibition on gay scouts and same-sex marriage and adoption rights, and would be focusing on issues similar to those covered in history and sociology. The ruling in the case found that the Salt Lake City School District (Cynthia L. Seidel in her official capacity as Assistant Superintendent of the district was the named defendant in the case) had made a "no narrowing" rule that only applied to PRISM and had required that PRISM fully engage whatever curricular area they were claiming connection to, rather than only address LGBT issues. The court pointed out that the "no narrowing" rule had not been required of the Students Against Drunk Driving or the Polynesian Club, two groups that had very well defined goals that, while they related to curricula, did not do so in the comprehensive way required of PRISM. In other words, the district was using an implicit rule in judging PRISM's application but not applying that implicit rule to any other application. The court disagreed with district objections that ruling for PRISM would mean making a closed forum impossible; instead, the court found the district could continue a closed forum but nonetheless had to apply its criteria fairly.

In other areas, schools have used their abstinence-only sexuality education policy to justify prohibiting groups that are sexuality-oriented, stating that the proposed Gay-Straight Alliance would, in the opinion of school leaders, violate the "well being and disruption" exceptions allowed by the EAA (*Caudillo v. Lubbock Independent School District*, 2004). At the time students requested a GSA at Lubbock High School, same-sex sodomy was still illegal in Texas, although the landmark case outlawing sodomy as unconstitutional, *Lawrence v. Texas* (2003) had already been heard by the Supreme Court and the ruling in *Caudillo v. Lubbock* came after the Supreme Court ruling in *Lawrence*. Nonetheless, the district used both the illegality of homosexual sex and the assertion that discussing gay rights violated the abstinence-only policy. The judge ruled for the district, arguing that there was no case law on this particular combination of abstinence-only policy, GSA, and EAA. Further, because an early flier used by the group had a web link that led to another page with web links that eventually led to sex-related information, the judge characterized the information associated with the GSA as "obscene, indecent, and lewd sexual material"

(*Caudillo v. Lubbock*, 2004, fn 5). This particular strategy for prohibiting GSAs was taken up by state legislators in Arizona and Utah, who proposed legislation banning sex-related student clubs. Other districts have taken a milder but also disrespectful tactic of asking students to call their GSA something else, like the "diversity club" (Horne, 2001).

As this brief history of the purpose of the EAA and the district responses to it show, the same issues raised in Congressional debate—whether young people can legally talk about sexuality and whether the First Amendment already protects their rights to do so—are still characterizing responses to GSAs and the EAA. In 2011 the Flour Bluff school district in Texas briefly cancelled all student extracurricular groups, including the Fellowship of Christian Athletes, in order to avoid approving a GSA. Only the intercession of the ACLU led to a reinstatement of all groups and the provisional acceptance of the GSA (Texas GSA Network, 2011). Knowing the guiding policy can sometimes, at least initially, encourage districts to avoid providing truly equal access. But my hope in this section is to show that students are energetic advocates for their own freedoms and that courts most often rule in favor of GSAs. While organizing a GSA and being part of changing district policy can be a fine way to learn about constitutional protections, it also takes tremendous energy and commitment. Watching GSAs try to organize, run into administrative or community obstacles, and re-energize themselves to advocate for district nondiscrimination policies and inclusion in something as minor as the high school yearbook is both inspiring and, to a certain extent, dispiriting. The youth who want to improve their schools have much more to do besides educating adults who should be looking after their well-being, and such activism takes its toll, as does living under restrictive laws or even reforms that are up for debate. Darcy White and Rob Stephenson (2013) have found that the stresses associated with living in areas where gay rights are up for public debate is associated with more health risks among gay men than in areas where legal protections are already in place. Further, they cite other studies indicating the health risks associated with stigmatization:

> In recent years, the rights of gay, lesbian, and bisexual individuals have been called into question by scores of initiatives and referenda, which create stigma and stress (Fingerhut, Riggle, & Rostosky, 2011). Conversely, legislation that validates same-sex relationships and extends rights and protections has been shown to have a positive impact on well-being, providing a sense of social inclusion and legitimacy (Fingerhut et al., 2011; Hatzenbuehler, Keyes, & Hasin, 2009). Policies that communicate equality and acceptance help define social norms and have wide-reaching implications, not only for the mental health and rights of sexual minorities but also for the future trajectory of the HIV epidemic. (White & Stephenson, 2013, p. 10)

But GSAs provide LGBTQ and ally youth with the space to engage critically with these obstacles and plan ways to intervene. J. B. Mayo (2013) argues that GSAs are spaces particularly in need of critical pedagogical approaches that provide youth with the tools to assess and respond to the key issues they face in schools and communities. He argues further that adult support in engaging the acts of reflection and transformation are critical to the success of such groups and that teacher preparation needs to involve critical pedagogical approaches to ensure teachers are able to work well in these roles.

THE DAY OF SILENCE:
RESISTANCE AND RECONCILIATION (HOPEFULLY)

Transformative projects are being developed by youth, either through GSAs or by other students to point out silences and possibilities for change within their schools. In Madison, Wisconsin, the GSA at one middle school, tired of hearing "that's so gay," created posters, funded by the school district, that read, "I just heard you say 'That's so gay.' What I think you meant was . . . " followed by a long list of adjectives like *ridiculous, silly, absurd,* and *foolish* (Kilman, 2007). The posters were handed out to all the teachers in the school, and because of this attention to the issue, the frequency of the comments dropped. Interrupting speech is not the only approach LGBTQ youth and their allies have taken to interrupt institutional, peer, and school personnel homophobia. The Day of Silence is a yearly activity, begun by college students but now also popular at high schools, wherein students pledge to remain silent for the duration of the school day to protest curricular and policy silences that omit information about and consideration of LGBTQ people. Students carry cards explaining the reason for their silence and usually organize "speak outs" at the end of the day to talk about their experiences. In addition, activities may include posters in schools highlighting important incidents and figures in LGBTQ history. The activity itself is meant to highlight silence but in fact the supporting materials distributed by students fill in gaps effectively.

The silence of student activists is also meant to stimulate questions that are generally not asked by other students and to encourage students and teachers who are not participating to begin to question their own silences on LGBTQ issues. This is an effective activity because while it does provide some answers in the form of cards or posters, it also encourages those observing to think further about the policy context of their schools, local and state laws, and the day-to-day activities that feel like silencing to the activists but may go unnoticed by the larger school community. The silence is, in effect, an opening and an invitation to reconsider what school feels like to those who experience education as a process of silencing. Their intentional silence

marks out that pervasive absence, and by all wearing the same clothes, usually black T-shirts, and sometimes duct-taping their mouths, students are
out in schools in a way that shows at least some of the number of students
affected by the silencing. As students pass out cards or pin ribbons onto other
students who have shown interest in the issues of LGBTQ youth, the sym-
bolic markers of those affected by institutional silencing grow. In some ways,
too, the Day of Silence is a way to express anger and withdrawal from school
communities that have not provided adequate support, information, or space
for LGBTQ communities. Student activists are both present in school, going
through their normal day, and also marking out their absence from regular discussion. They also mark out the extent to which they unintentionally
pass as heterosexual in schools or usually remain silent about their LGBTQ
identity, that is, the action of remaining intentionally silent draws into question the institutional silencing of their usual speech, showing that there have
been times when they did not speak out. In the use of silence as a message,
students indicate that they are still not able to speak about LGBTQ issues out
loud in schools during regular classes. In most places, the end of the school
day signals a shift in the demonstration, and students in the action and students interested in what it meant gather to talk in more detail. It is also not
uncommon for Day of Silence participants to break their silence during the
day if someone is really interested in what is going on.

Like other attempts to counter school-based homophobia, this activity has
met with resistance, including a nationally organized Day of Truth the day after the Day of Silence. The organizer of that activity withdrew his support for
it, concerned it was too confrontational, after a number of high-profile youth
suicides, including Tyler Clementi's, about two weeks before that year's Day of
Truth underscored to him the high costs of homophobia (Gilgoff, 2010). Focus
on the Family has since taken up the Day of Truth, now renamed as the Day
of Dialogue, to help students get to a "deeper and freer" conversation about
sexuality and to "stand up for those being harmed or bullied while offering the
light of what God's Word says" (Focus on the Family, 2013). The end to an an-
tagonistic response is just one indication that youth are having a major impact
even on conservative organizing.

Even more recently, Exodus International, an organization advocating that
gay people become heterosexual, has disbanded. Its leadership has apologized
for the damaging effects of its attempts to alter people's sexual orientation and
for the negative judgment on gayness related that project. As their leader, Alan
Chambers (2013) explained, "It is strange to be someone who has both been
hurt by the church's treatment of the LGBT community, and also be someone
who must apologize for being part of the very system of ignorance that perpet-
uated that hurt." Explaining in his apology that his own same-sex attractions
have continued, Chambers adds:

I am sorry that some of you spent years working through the shame and guilt you felt when your attractions didn't change. I am sorry we promoted sexual orientation change efforts and reparative theories about sexual orientation that stigmatized parents. I am sorry that there were times I didn't stand up to people publicly "on my side" who called you names like sodomite—or worse. I am sorry that I, knowing some of you so well, failed to share publicly that the gay and lesbian people I know were every bit as capable of being amazing parents as the straight people that I know. I am sorry that when I celebrated a person coming to Christ and surrendering their sexuality to Him that I callously celebrated the end of relationships that broke your heart. I am sorry that I have communicated that you and your families are less than me and mine.

Increasingly, too, conservative groups working against same-sex marriage are indicating that generational changes in attitude about LGBTQ people mean that broader political changes, like the recent end to federal aspects of DOMA and the restarting of same-sex marriage in California, will continue. Youth activism and the younger generation's great familiarity with LGBTQ issues and greater likelihood of knowing someone LGBTQ are a key part of this cultural shift in favor of gay rights (Burke, 2013).

LGBTQ YOUTH AND PUBLIC SPACES

LGBTQ youth also challenge homophobia in their more subtle decisions to represent themselves and create LGBTQ-friendly spaces out of everyday public space. In her work on LGBTQ youth of color in a community center, Mollie Blackburn (2004, 2005) shows how young gay men of color and young gender nonconforming men of color maintain their sense of connection with one another in urban public spaces through use of language and gesture. They understand both the need to challenge their felt exclusions from such spaces but also the need to maintain a sense of cohesion. The scenes of interaction she describes would be legible to outsiders as young people taking space for their own, but the specific meaning would not always be evident. Such activities, not uncommon to youth in general, show a complex interaction between being out with a peer group, being public but not necessarily understandable to adults present, and also maintaining a safe distance from potential harm in public.

Mary L. Gray (2007) shows a more spectacular version of taking space in rural areas where young LGBTQ people go to Wal-Mart or Christian bookstores after their meetings in drag. After meeting at a community center in an LGBTQ group, members would go out to a local Wal-Mart in drag, posing and taking photos of themselves in the aisles, understanding that their presence as potential consumers would help legitimize their presence. They knew, too, that they had friends who worked at the store who would be able to defend their right to use the space for their impromptu drag shows and spectacularity. They posted photos of these excursions on their website and reported that those images were the most heavily visited part of their site, so together with their ability to change what might be expected at the local megastore and the circulation of the images of queerness in an unexpected location, their change of the scene worked in multiple ways.

Youth have other considerations when thinking about their sexual identity or negotiating the degree to which they will publicly express that identity. In their study of Latino youth, Yon-Leau and Muñoz-Laboy (2010) describe the complex interaction between respecting the resources for identity related to their ethnic background and understanding particular social contexts of the meaning of their identities. Examining Latino youth who draw on cultural resources for thinking about their bisexuality and sexual minority status, they found youth who were exhausted by labels and youth who complexified labels, including "confused lesbian" and "nonstraight" (p. 108). They also found a careful analysis of the cultural, ethnic, and religious context went into deciding how to act and appear. One young woman felt that there was a balance between wanting to be out and wanting to show understanding of cultural and religious beliefs of the people in her family and community:

> You have to have respect. I wouldn't go around kissing another girl knowing the way our world is pretty much, and how everyone sees gays and lesbians, and how some people are disgusted by it, and just don't like it, and religion and all that stuff. So I wouldn't do it. I don't care if it's a group or a gay party and you're just making out with a girl, I don't care or it's just a group of gay people and two girls are making out, who cares. But when you do it in front of people you know don't like it, then I feel that's disrespectful. You have to have some respect. (Yon-Leau & Muñoz-Laboy, 2010, p. 111)

The decision to act and appear in ways that both respect ethnic bonds and also respond to particular school contexts helped one young Puerto Rican LGBTQ student move through schools with identities varying from butch lesbian to female to male (Mayo, 2007). Her preferred pronoun was usually female but she also had strong bonds with other Puerto Rican young men in her school and community and would hide men's clothes to change into either for school or for socializing outside of her home. While she did have friendships with female preservice teacher education students who worked at the local Latina/o community center, nonetheless, her choice of public gender presentation was often male to more easily fit into the ethnic, linguistic, and sexuality-related peer group she most desired to be with, sometimes bringing girlfriends along too. Their negotiations of such spaces are also evidently as complex.

The ability, willingness, and sometimes need for such flexibilities indicates the textured way in which young LGBTQ people, especially people of color or gender nonconforming youth, read and understand what is possible in any given space or interaction. LGBTQ youth of color maintain their ties to home racial and ethnic communities, knowing full well that those communities provide resources against White racism and also simply out of the joy of living and being in communities that provide meaning and support to them. Rejection from sustaining communities for any LGBTQ young person is challenging, and rejection from a minority community potentially even more so. On the one hand, these dexterous transitions among identity categories related to gender or sexuality are indications of commitment to stay and be with one's community, but on the other hand, such felt need to change represents an understanding that such communities may reject gender or sexual minorities.

Youth in schools, families, communities, and public spaces also quickly learn what is acceptable where, who might help them appear in particular ways, and who will reject them. Because they both understand these complexities and also need to access their education, it is all the more imperative that schools recognize the work they put into their strategies and commitment to identities and communities and provide ways for them to continue that creativity and get through school. Whether spectacular, subtle, or shifting, LGBTQ youth are in all schools, in expected and unexpected places. They know to watch carefully for signs of support; they know to demand outrageously for inclusion; and they also work and change our understandings of key categories of identity or refuse identity altogether. As some forms of LGBTQ relationships and communities gain recognition, it is important that we not limit what comes next but help ensure that education can be something of a resource to newer generations continuing to work on older problems of exclusion and promises of possibility.

CHAPTER 6

LGBTQ Online Communities and Support

This chapter discusses the increasing role of online communities and other forms of new media for providing LGBT and ally youth with context in which to make connections, express identities, and provide a sense of community support, even if they do not feel supported by their local, geographical community. Drawing on recent studies of youth participation in online communities, this examines how LGBT and ally–related concerns may be more readily expressed—and information necessary to LGBT and ally youth may be more readily accessed—online than in face-to-face settings. Like the extracurricular activities detailed in the previous chapter, this chapter shows youth resiliency and creativity in spaces too often defined only by their potential for risk or cyberbullying. By making virtual or mixing virtual and face-to-face communities away from harassment in schools or disapproval of particular identities in nonvirtual spaces, online and other new media spaces provide LGBT and ally youth with new tools for voicing their concerns and creating educational and socially supportive expressive community. In addition, this chapter addresses the concerns of rural youth, whose use of online community can either augment the resources they find locally or exacerbate their feeling of distance from images of LGBTQ youth online.

LGBTQ youth find queer community in cyberspace, supplementing or even supplanting geographical community. As they do, they develop critical understandings of representation and the limitations of virtual communities. There has been a longstanding relationship between queer people and technological innovation, from the growth of industry that enabled the formation of communities organized around sexual and gender minority identities and activities in the 20th century (D'Emilio, 1983) to the development of a vast variety of cyber communities starting before the turn of the 21st ("Cyber Queers," 1996). As Lori MacIntosh and Mary Bryson (2008) argue, studying queer online communities gives a way to view LGBTQ youth not by what they lack, but by what they find and create in new cyberspaces. Such online engagement may facilitate the development of virtual identities and/or create both virtual and face-to-face spaces for engagement. The virtual and real may be neither separate nor distinct. Technologically enhanced forms of communication maintain social networks through linked proximities like IM and chatrooms and the now ubiquitous social network sites, refigure what counts as living space, or simply provide the tools to organize and maintain face-to-face relationships. Virtual discussions can themselves become "place" or "home," as Joyce Y. M. Nip has found in her study of the Hong Kong lesbian site, Queer Sisters (Nip, 2004). Cyberspace can also be used to augment and shift identities in ways less possible in other contexts, as Susan Driver (2007) has discussed concerning the flexible and innovative gender and sexuality identity play she has observed online. In his discussion of the importance of queer friendship and thinking about the meanings of sexuality in Asian contexts, John Nguyet Erni (2003) argues that "queer youths' passion for the Internet" is clear from "Singapore, Taiwan, the Philippines, Korea, and Hong Kong [where] they have reported on the enormous usefulness of the Internet not only to make queer friends, but also to question and debate sexual politics" (p. 382). Queer youth in the United States increasingly find images of themselves through participation in online communities whether or not they also have a face-to-face LGBTQ community as well. And as Fann's (2005) discussion of the Chinese context shows, LGBTQ youth in the United States and elsewhere may also find that without a large enough community in which to be out in their local, real space, youth can experience being out only online.

LGBTQ DIGITAL DIVIDES

Just as social commentators may have simultaneously over- and underemphasized what the telephone would do to human interaction, likewise the cyber revolution has changed habits of action and thinking both drastically and, then again, not so much. Despite the proliferation of emerging hybrid spaces and relations, there is also a new sort of digital divide being created between those queer youth whose access to cyber-queer spaces give them the ability to discover and create new forms of queerness and those queer youth whose experience of surveillance or lack of access to technology leave them outside of these new circuits of identity, representation, and communities. Although the digital divides structured by race, class, and disability continue, schools may provide some help in alleviating those (Trotter, 2006); but the school context does not provide help to queers of all colors, races, genders, and abilities who find themselves unable to engage with and create queer content in the presence of web filters and adult supervision.

Giving attention to this kind of queer digital divide must remain tied to attention to the diversity of queer communities and the proliferation of queer spaces on the Web. To continue to only see the space of the Web from the perspective of those who can easily inhabit it simply reinforces those divides. At the same time that it is crucial to ask questions about who can access technologically mediated spaces, it is also educationally important to teach more critically about technology use. At one end of this cyber-life spectrum of digital possibilities are youth-created (if sometimes adult-moderated) innovative sites that take representation to its limits and create new arrays of identities and identifications (Driver, 2006, 2007). But on the other end of this spectrum is technology's role in facilitating social-hierarchy-as-usual, through continuation of already existing racism, sexism, homophobia, and transphobia. Cyberspace, Lisa Nakamura (2000) has argued, can provide a context in which to play out problematic forms of identity masquerade and "tourism," given that online conversations and role-playing valorize dabbling in racial and ethnic identity, but disparage those who bring up race and ethnicity as issues for serious discussion (p. 712). When posters either conform to dominant norms around race, gender, sexuality, and so on, or when the majority of those setting the terms of online representation simply replicate existing hierarchies, the promise of queering cyberspace can fade into tired, old, commercial, overmediated, glossy, mainstream sites unconcerned with their roles in maintaining raced, classed, and regional forms of digital divide. LGBTQ youth of color, in addition to experiencing homophobia and transphobia online, had a 19% chance of experiencing racism during their participation in mediated chats and a 59% chance of so doing during participation in unmediated chats on the Internet (Tynes, Reynolds, & Greenfield, 2004). Harp, Bachman, Rosas-Moreno, and Loke (2010) found that African American youth were more likely than other groups of young people to use the Internet to think through politics and organize for civic change and improvement.

Those who can access technology learn how to use cyberculture to begin to form face-to-face or virtual relationships, learning how to negotiate consent, attraction, and political action through the myriad sites available, understanding as they do so that representation itself complicates what it is they are seeing and with whom they are interacting. Experience with online communication helps them understand that people are never as simple as their self-representations. They learn this or have it reinforced by drawing on not only their own experience of hiding their sexuality in virtual and real spaces, but also by reading about warnings about correspondence on the Web posted by other users. They understand as well that representation itself is a shifting and uncertain experience requiring close reading, double messages, and ultimately uncertainty. LGBTQ youth may know much about this dynamic from their flirtations with seemingly straight peers whose straightness seems less than certain (McCready, 2010). They also say they understand the instability of what queerness is from their tentative attempts to find others who are queer like them, but whom they find out to be queer in very different ways than they might have expected.

A few of the rural queer youth, including straight and LGBT people, I interviewed in 2007 also pointed out that images of gay urban life, whether observed in the mass media or reflected in cyberspace, were not useful to them. They could not find transportation to get them to the city and because they were more comfortable in rural settings generally, they did not necessarily want to have to go to a city to find other queers. Nor were they interested in the stylistic markers and commodified LGBTQ identities they saw reflected in mass media representations. The class and regional implications of both the sleek, fashionable gay man and his twinned metrosexual straight friend who is as interested in fashion and grooming as any stereotyped gay man is, did not necessarily hold appeal for rural young people, some of whom have characterized themselves as more comfortable in shopping at Big R or Farm and Fleet than in the kind of stores and salons they see on fashion-based reality TV. One of my conversations with rural queer youth circled around the images of farm implements in school mascots, reinforcing a sense that these young people were conversant in technologies rooted in another area and not particularly drawn to innovations that did not reflect their particular desires for community and activity. Urban styles and queerness were linked in media images in a way that did not reflect their lives. Such representations of queer lives were simply quite beyond them, neither proximate nor within their realm of interest. Even those who waited until they went to college to find queer community said they chose small, relatively rural universities understanding that while they wanted some change, they wanted to meet other small-town queers.

While there are significant ways in which digital community can supplement local community or even provide community to students unable to easily meet other LGBTQ youth, most of the rural queer youth felt that they could not even safely use the Web to explore LGBTQ cultures elsewhere and that that kind of queer life would have to wait until they left their small towns. Given studies of queer youth that do find rural young people able to access queer community on the Web (Gray, 2007), it may simply be that those I interviewed were more drawn to face-to-face community, with a few exceptions, or had diminished expectations about what they might find online because they had only limited access to the Web. But whether they accessed the Web or were able to speculate about queer representation in the mass media, they all knew that there were more possibilities out there than they found in their local schools. Like the students who have reported in other interviews that they never would have joined a gay group in their high school, knowing such things were there made all the difference and made waiting for a time they felt comfortable to express their sexuality seem like it was time spent waiting for something that was already happening near them. In other words, a large component of waiting is active and enables the person waiting to engage in pleasurable speculation about possibilities. The space of waiting, then, is a space of contemplation, drawing together the hints about queer culture gleaned from popular images, out queers, and even knowledge that there simply are queer people meeting with one another somewhere, however unknown the actual contours of that community are. But because they literally live at some distance from urban queers, that city LGBTQ life is not exactly what they are after. It is because of its urbanity, a normalized space of consumption and mobility, a life more easily observed in mass media than the rural life, and while they did not refer to themselves as non-normative in the edgier sense of queerness, it is clear that their inclination to remain rural is a rejection of the city. It would certainly do to remain wary of the rejection of the city standing in for an embrace of racial homogeneity, but the desire to remain in place is also a rejection of the queer norm of mobility, class or otherwise.

A few rural queer youth remarked that by not having queer community in close proximity, they were drawn to other minority people in their schools. One self-identified queer White heterosexual woman became best friends with the only person in her school, as far as they initially knew, who was gay. That friendship dyad also immediately made friends with the first Black student to move into their community, all of them brought together by their understanding of their difference from everyone else but equally aware of their differences from one another. While this is too small an example to draw a generalization from, this creation of a queer group with little in common except lack of commonality from others did have an effect on other people in the school who began to make subtle gestures of connection with this trio. As the young woman explained, other students wanted her friends to know that they too did not fit into the norm as well as might be expected, and so by creating a small collection of outsiders, the group itself acted as an organizing point for others who wanted a sense of community that was not mainstream, but also was not distinctly defined as queer in the more specific sense of sexuality and gender identity. The group, though, did provide other students with a place to try out coming out or at least to express hints that they might be thinking about coming out. In addition, the "queer" trio found themselves the recipients of positively valenced gossip about who else might benefit from being with them. In short, they became a hub of queer and quasi-queer communication in their school, though they also received negative attention as well. In contrast, rural or nonmetropolitan LGBTQ adults, according to Oswald and Culton (2003), find their locations largely supportive as long as they are not too open about their sexuality, but such communities became highly stressful as a result of inaccessible support or overt homophobia. According to Holman and Oswald (2011) most LGBTQ parents in nonmetropolitan areas found teachers to be supportive and found, too, that they were able to make connections with day care workers and educators on the basis of shared parenting rather than differences in sexuality. Holman and Oswald also found that LGBTQ parents met with educators able to acknowledge them as same-sex parents, encouraging children, for instance, to show artwork to both of their mothers, and that small-town educators were also willing to provide support against bullying. Such research complicates the picture of rural life, while also showing that in other kinds of interactions, LGBTQ issues may still pose challenges for a sense of community.

LGBTQ YOUTH, CYBER PRESENCE, AND INTENTIONAL COMMUNITY

In her study of rural LGBTQ youth, Mary L. Gray (2007) provides examples of young people, including AJ, a female-to-male transteen, who literally spoke softly in public but whose exuberance and confidence was expressed in his website. AJ described the development of his website, chronicling his transition and providing information to other transyouth, as a reaction to the limitations of other websites with which he had experience. Finding them either too restrictive in the range of information they provided or because content was behind a paywall, he "wanted to give people all the free pictures and info I could" (p. 54). His move into the public, then, was both a critique and reaction against the thinness of materials he had already found there and also created for him a place to be more specific and communicative about his experiences. Further, by enabling him to share photos of his bodily changes and sound files of his voice shift while undergoing transition, AJ was able to create a sense of presence and embodied detail in his representations, another way of mitigating the potential distance of his online relationships with readers. His website also contained responses from friends and family, indicating to readers interested in transition that he was embedded in a supportive community and providing them with the opportunity to join this already-existing support network for their own transition. Not only did AJ's site draw in local commentary, he developed international contacts and support as well. Gray (2007) argues that the bolstering effects of his growing online community allowed AJ to create a new public sense of himself.

Hillier and Harrison (2007) found that lesbian, gay, and bisexual youth were more likely to find the sorts of support AJ found online than in their face-to-face communities. Other researchers have found that accessing health-related information online enables LGB students to more readily access health services in their local communities, bolstered as they are with information ahead of time and a better idea of what to expect (Ybarra & Suman, 2008). Similarly, youth may practice coming out online in order to gauge the reactions they might get, distance themselves from negative reactions, or prefer to do so in supportive spaces rather than challenging face-to-face contexts (Hillier, Mitchell, & Ybarra, 2012). One respondent to Hillier et al. (2012) explained,

"Coming out in person is so awkward because you never know how that person is going to react. Online is easier because if someone isn't OK with it, you don't have to see the disgust on his face" (p. 235). Another noted that negative judgments did not cause them as much concern, explaining, "We aren't worried about rejection or judgment if we can't see the person we're talking to" (p. 234). Whether online communities and connections become their main sources of support or whether online connections give LGBTQ students a chance to try out information-seeking activities or developing personal relationships through coming out or dating, such new spaces for exploration of ideas, identities, and information helps provide the missing resources in local and school communities.

The Internet is also a potentially safer space for young LGBTQ people to try out same-sex attractions, without fear of what asking for a phone number or indicating interest in a partner might mean in a geographical space (Hillier & Harrison, 2007). While the Internet has generated cultural fears of pedophilia and sexual exploitation, young people also note that it has given them much broader freedoms to think in complex ways about who they are and who they want to be thought of when they are in communication with others. Drawing on ideas, too, about the erosion between the virtual and the real (Stone, 1995; Turkle, 1997), LGBTQ youth see their participation in both spaces as linked but also potentially affording different experiences, neither of which are more authentic than the other and neither of which show a truer sense of who they are (Hillier & Harrison, 2007). LGBTQ youth also indicated that there were differences in their self-presentation online, precisely because it gave them a place to loosen up and not have to be completely accurate about themselves (Hillier & Harrison, 2007). Hillier and Harrison (2007) note that this same ability to practice and try out heterosexuality has been a feature of what straight youth do in face-to-face settings and in how they use the Internet, but the added benefit for LGBTQ youth is the relative freedom from negative responses. Vicki Fraser (2010) suggests that such online explorations offer LGBTQ youth a new kind of closet, one that does not replicate the pressures of exclusions of the old form of the closet, but instead shows the vibrancy and creativity of a community that can form in places without the surveillance of homophobia and transphobia in face-to-face communities. The closet on the Internet is an active space of communicating and building new meanings (Fraser, 2010).

Susan Driver (2007) suggests that online communities are particularly adept at collaborative approaches, helping young lesbians and other women push at their understandings of gender and relationship, even challenge one another, but still maintain connection. Moreover, Driver stresses the "intentionality" of such developing communities, arguing that both the exclusions experienced in face-to-face settings push young LGBTQ youth to find community elsewhere and that their participation in online communities requires more active choice, thought, and reflection (p. 173). Driver (2007) and Bury (2005) also note that communities based on the Internet work within persistent dilemmas of exclusion and inclusion, aware of the boundaries they create but also critical of their own tendencies to do so. The flexibility of movement between sites and the possibilities afforded by relatively quick shifts in ideas, identities, and communities allows young people a greater range of expressive and identificatory positions to try out. Their awareness of their own tactics, whether of exclusion or the degree of control they have over their self-representation in terms of use of names, pronouns, or sites to participate in, shows both their interest in complexity of identity and the possibilities of the medium in which they are communicating.

CRITICAL MEDIA LITERACY AND CYBER NORMALIZATION

For those youth who are able to access the Web without surveillance, websites like AJ's provide additional insights into forms of gender and sexual identity that they might otherwise have not encountered locally. In addition, that experience of seeing the diversities of queer possibility also taught them the limitations of mass culture and school-based representations of gayness. They may also practice creative reading against the grain or pick up hints about characters and plots that are not always evident or further develop to their own satisfactions augmented readings of those images that are clearly LGBTQ (Driver, 2007). Gay youth are also more likely than heterosexual youth to understand the limitations of sexuality education and health education in public schools and fill in those missing lessons by turning to Internet sources (Mustanski, Lyons, & Garcia, 2011). LGBTQ youth, too, may find school lessons begin to raise questions about sexual health but do not supply enough information or those lessons are not sufficiently developed and repeated to be effective, and so they use the Internet, in effect, to find out more and also to be reminded of what they learned in a one-time school assembly on HIV (DeHaan, Kuper, Magee, Bigelow, & Mustanski, 2013).

This younger generation's analysis of television reruns that indicate what an earlier generation may have taken as at least a gesture toward better representation indicates that participation in social media and popular media can help start a critical awareness of what images and circulation of those images might mean. Like the earlier LGBTQ people doing research on their own communities, reading and discussing novels, and analyzing how representation of gay characters reflected social and cultural pressures or openings, young people are also critical media consumers and analysts. Contemporary popular culture, too, provides youth with ways to rethink and represent complex identities, whether reworking and creating hip-hop (Love, 2012) or queerly engaging media

(Lipton, 2008). Such critical media literacy also helps LGBTQ and ally youth chart the shifts in those representations of LGBTQ people across the last few decades as the Internet is a new archive of social and political understandings. In some ways, then, the ability to search out historical information of the recent past or older media content provide youth with a way to critique what came before and give them insight, as well, into persistent exclusions. As they expand their critical analysis into the production of media itself, they sometimes find the same high production values and limited range of images that characterize mainstream media are also reflected in high-profile gay sites. LGBTQ websites, for instance, may not be much of an improvement over the glossy images on mainstream TV; as one early critic of such sites put it, a "commercial spirit embodies" the design of LGBTQ web presence:

> These hip, young multicultural types are the on-screen icons who lead us into the site. They're undeniably attractive, but their images seem like false advertising, especially when you enter the Real Life section that features entertaining stories of fizzled romances and other woes of modern gay life. (Helfand, 1996)

Other queer youth have pointed out that queer youth sites are informationally helpful but perhaps a little too close to school-like messages. They point to a kind of cyber normalization reflected in some queer youth websites. Caught between a desire for relevancy to youth concerns and a concern they will be seen as not legitimate or be made inaccessible because of web-filtering software, websites for queer youth sometimes balance discussions about sexuality while prohibiting the use of web chats for what might be seen as sexual purposes. There are, of course, numerous reasons for this enforced reticence: concern that adults will sexually exploit queer youth, concern that whole areas of sexuality information will be censored, and concern that certain kinds of talk are not appropriate to the context of information and activism. Other kinds of websites and chats likely dispute this disconnect between sexuality information and sexuality, but there are a variety of websites that push the public, squeaky-clean face of queer youth, likely to maintain an image of professionalism for the website sponsors and show the legitimacy of queer youth sites in the current context of web filtering. Ironically, though, even the very professional and legitimate sex information sites still find themselves filtered out of public school and public library computers (just as breast cancer sites continue to be blocked by overly sensitive surveillance software in schools and libraries).

Many queer youth sites are, then, mediated spaces or what Gray (2007) calls "boundary publics" (p. 53), helping create something like an LGBTQ youth public space but also maintaining strategies of safety in local communities, while creating broader connections in online community. Some are clearly under adult supervision or maintain limited access policies to outsiders or those who are overage. In some cases, this means a social worker monitors communication among queer youth and weeds out problematic posts. When I began collecting information on queer youth sites in the mid-1990s, it was not uncommon to find sites that very clearly drew the line between legitimate talk for that site and talk that belonged elsewhere. For instance, one site, while it still had an interactive forum (disabled by 2013), encouraged its users to "Please *DO* feel free to discuss any aspect of your feelings or experiences regarding sexuality, but . . . Do *NOT* post solicitations for sex—real, virtual, or telephonic. . . . Do *NOT* post pornography or links to pornography—not that we think anything is wrong with porn, this just isn't the place for it" (Coalition for Positive Sexuality, 1996, 2008). This particular site is notable for its not having had a moderator, only a maintainer, so the sternly worded request is intended as the main check on content. Given that the site provides accurate and well-framed information on sexuality for youth, it is also likely that their stern warning is meant to keep a clear division between sex education and other sexual possibilities. Clearly they are not disparaging other forms of sexual communication, simply marking out the limits for their website (and perhaps indicating the difficulties of those limits). They have since shut down this interactive feature citing too much spam, another indication of the tension between content and commodification on the Internet (Coalition for Positive Sexuality, 2013). In other instances, queer youth themselves monitor content, and importantly, try to keep the spaces free from unwanted adult intervention. But especially in the cases of websites run by social service organizations or youth advocacy groups, not only is the legitimacy of the group tied to the content of the chats, but grants and professional standards require such limitations.

Whatever restrictions sites may have, they do provide information that is lacking in school contexts. In short, while youth sites may appear quite normalized and mediated, they are still radical when compared with most public school curricula. HIV education and information on the varieties of sexualities and coming out processes are available on most queer youth sites. While a site like the Gay, Lesbian & Straight Education Network spends little time on HIV education, it offers many resources for coming out, Gay-Straight Alliances, and school-related activism. The public face of queer youth, then, is perhaps constrained by the legitimacy sought by political organizers of all ages but also provides queer youth and their allies—even youth who may be skeptical of the faces of models on the sites—with tools and support to work against the exclusions they experience in schools and communities.

But the glossy images of happy multicultural queer youth on website homepages have drawn critical commentary from youth, ranging from comments about how well groomed and thin everyone appears to be and how perpetually cheerful they all appear. Youth are not concerned that LGBTQ people are portrayed in a positive light, but rather that the images are too staged and predictable. A few young LGBTQ and ally organizers have remarked that they feel they are getting propaganda materials from national organizations, though at the same time they have used those materials to organize. In part, LGBTQ and ally youth may be sorting through their own divergent experiences while reading these images, balancing both their school success with the home challenges they have faced, too. While they excel at school and are youth leaders, they have also raised difficult issues of substance abuse, incarceration, abandonment by parents, and complete alienation from the school environment, even while still attending and still working to improve their schools. The youth prominent in social service websites that draw their criticism appear most often to be leaders, well-schooled in the rhetoric of organization and capable of facing their difficulties down. They are a testament to the organizations they represent and doubtless ideal figures for youth visiting the sites, though they also personify a commodified image of an ideal young LGBTQ person.

While the transformative potential of the Internet, in terms of widespread access and "play" among identities has been prominently discussed in terms of adult queer sites and usage, "queer" in the context of social service–sponsored sites sometimes appears to mark either uncertainty of identity or the link among youth sexualities, rather than a critique of normative sexuality. As much as sites may try to remain open to variety and possibility, because they are rooted in representation, there is a point where descriptions fail to capture all possibility, and thus the sites, by including particular forms of queerness, inadvertently reinforce the limitations of the concept. Elise Paradise (2008), working on researching queer youth in cyberspace, argues that in surveys this kind of "boxing" of identity is a constant concern and that queer youth themselves, in her experience, are frustrated with the limitations of categories and well able to suggest missing possibilities (p. 9). Such a critique of limitations of online surveys and other research from gender nonconforming youth is also evident in GLSEN's (2013b) discussion of the responses they were unable to include in their study because some of their respondents combined identity categories in innovative ways that refused to comply with the protocols of the study and the commonplace understandings of how such categories like gender and transgender identity are thought to relate.

Even given the limitations of many sites, forms of identification and lingering exclusions, there are other ways to read the queer potential of even high production value sites. Read by those expecting queers to be nothing but trouble, the glossy images are themselves queering any idea that risk and trauma are the lot of queer youth. Indeed, the proliferation of queer youth sites for information exchange, political organizing, and socializing all underscore the vast shift away from queer youth as a social services–mediated group. Sites are run by youth and for youth, and while there are still links about substance abuse and safer sex, the dominant tone is confident, welcoming, and well schooled in its own complexities of subculture and spaces—cyber or otherwise—in which to meet and greet.

THE LINK MADE FLESH

That the Internet might provide such a nonmediated space for queer youth has not gone unnoticed by school-based authorities wanting to limit such discussions among youth. The presence of a web link on a Gay-Straight Alliance poster, a link that led, as links do, beyond its main address into what the school district considered information inappropriate for youth, has been successfully used as part of a case justifying the prohibition of a GSA from meeting on school grounds. Using district abstinence-only policy as its rationale for ruling the GSA obscene, the judge spent a notable amount of time in his ruling discussing the lewdness of websites that could be reached by going a number of links away from the web address the alliance had originally provided as a link on its poster (*Caudillo v. Lubbock*, 2004). That queer youth knew the importance of the websites is evident in their initial decision to print a link in a nonlinkable medium like poster paper. They likely understood that they were disseminating not only a call to meet but an invitation into myriad queer possibilities, the web link beginning a kind of search that is not limited by the particular bodies and identities inhabiting particular school locations. The presence of the link also indicated to other youth who only had access to computers under surveillance that there were sites out there, and more than just that general knowledge, it provided them with one place to start, should they have the opportunity to do so. The link may have been particularly irksome to school officials because, as older people, their generation had not grown up as so-called net natives and thus their own lack of facility with the Internet may have raised their suspicions about what was being disseminated by this link (or their own particular web-based proclivities may have raised their suspicions). While that particular invitation into queer cyber life was part of the school's argument against their group, the group's tactic of enlarging the community represented by the flyer by positing a community bound together by web links is part of a new trend in youth organizing in general and points to the potential boundlessness of linking.

Understanding how links embody and disembody communities structures Jaqueline Rhodes's (2004) argument that hyperlinking is queer "not in where it starts or where it goes, but in its imminent possibility" (p. 388). Asserting that the "hypertext is an erotic textual moment, when idea and action collide," Rhodes theorizes that "queertext," the queer union of text and cyber possibility, can help explain both why the gay youth used the link and why the school prohibited both the link and the group (p. 389). By linking their own youth project to queer online and face-to-face communities, the students were asserting that they were themselves already part of other communities, including those communities the school authority considered oppositional and inappropriate. The administration clearly understood the web links to be indicative of how the word might be made flesh and that the bodies indicated by those links were perverse bodies. Because participation in online communities is also a way to begin to join a political or identity-based community (Gray, 2007; Nip, 2004; Russell, 2002), severing links between youth and online opportunities exacerbates the problem of distance between queer generations.

RETOOLING AND REASSEMBLING

Where youth are able to access and use technology, they may do so with more facility than adults and may create spaces and relations. As Ito et al. (2008) point out, new technologies do potentially upset the traditional adult-youth hierarchy given their facility with technological innovation and use. Web-tracking software can give queer youth ways to leave hints to friends and family about their sexual orientation, and policing of appropriate websites indicates that there is something queer out there to be found. Moments of adult surveillance, for cyber-savvy queer youth, can be shifted into new forms of communication.

Even queer youth not fully involved in social organizations use the queer cultures available on the Web for a variety of kinds of communication. A striking use of the Web and especially web-monitoring devices can be seen in one young man's decision to come out to his parents by visiting sites that would help parents deal with a child's coming out. He knew that he did not have complete freedom to use the family's home computer to explore web-based gay culture, something he instead did at cybercafés, but he was aware that cyber life has a communicative aspect even in indirect ways. He knew that his parents reviewed the history of web visits once he had gone to bed for the evening, and so before going to bed he visited a series of sites designed to help parents understand their gay children. His strategy gave them the time and space to understand his message and explore the web resources he had led them to, and it gave him time to rest before needing to have further conversation with his parents. Cyberculture became seamlessly woven into his strategies of communication, not as an eruption of ambiguity or celebration of technoculture, but simply what he did during the course of a day or a conservation. As Bryson, MacIntosh, Jordan, and Lin (2006) have argued, it is "quotidian" examples like this that push beyond the too easy celebration of cyberculture or too suspicious fears of "technological determinism" (p. 793).

This particular young man was equally savvy at corresponding and meeting with other young gay men in his area, men close enough to be able to visit but not part of his social circle at school (though he was out). In this sense, he used the distance allowed by cyberculture in order to maintain privacy in aspects of his queer life that diverged from his life as a socially and academically active and prominent student. Perhaps parallel to work in girls' studies that discusses the realm of privacy created by girls' social networks that are largely centered around their rooms or around public spaces where adults' presence may be minimal, this young gay man used a combination of web access in his private room and social contacts beyond his local circle to extend his range of privacy outward. That he was able to travel relatively freely meant that he could combine cyber relationships with face-to-face meetings. Other young people I spoke with in 2007 have remarked on the humorous disjuncture between their online relationships and the moment of face-to-face meeting, where blondes turn out to be brunettes, tall young men turn out to be shorter and older, and yet all who have related such stories understand that online self-representations are meant as a sort of enhanced version of the self, like flirtation. Susan Driver (2006) has argued that queer online communities may not find deception problematic "because the point is not to tell the truth, but rather to respond to others with understanding, care, and reciprocity" (p. 231).

In these situations, the cyber assembly is itself a proof against deception, and cyberspace becomes an intimate context where publicity can emphasize affective content. Nip (2004) has shown that the Queer Sisters online community provided what users felt was a public community necessary for emotional communication between love interests that was more trustworthy because it was in the company of other friends who could read it. In this case, cybercommunity is intensely personal and even intimate, pushing past the privacy of relationships into a more common space of recognition and communication than would likely be possible for people who can only "assemble" in cyberspace, not unlike the experience of holding hands while walking down hallways in high schools. Other youth have remarked that they find large groups online easier to come out in (Driver, 2006), suggesting that there may be a shift toward technology-enabled forms of public intimacy.

Queer youth also create these civic cyber-assembly spaces to discuss controversial issues that they feel cannot be openly addressed in other spaces (Russell, 2002). Groups like Gay-Straight Alliances are increasingly using online spaces for their own organizing purposes, behind password protections to maintain their group's privacy and develop cohesion, but meant for working on public projects. Other queer and postqueer uses of cyber assembly derive their energies from engagement across differences through social networking sites. Internet interaction is as much about creating sociability as it is about the exchange of information, so learning how to ethically engage and also how to critically analyze content and communications is crucial. As MacIntosh and Bryson (2008) argue, "Inasmuch as one's identity is formed through connection with un/like others, MySpace holds open the promise of multiple and complex relations of recognizability and connection" (p. 140). But as these new cyberspaces develop, older places still matter, given that the "geography of racial segregation and concentrated poverty" (Mossberger, Tolbert, & Gilbert, 2006, p. 584), as well as region, affect the ability of people of color and lower income people to access and use technology on their own terms (Hargittai, 2011). Expanding access becomes particularly crucial to the project of developing the critical analysis skills and the ability to form relations in/through difference. These are issues important to all young people as their lives are increasingly intertwined with online activities, but all the more important for gender and sexual minority youth who often find more support, and more outlets for their intellectual and creative development, in online spaces than in schools or families.

References

Aldrich, A. (1958/2006). *We, too, must love.* New York, NY: Feminist Press.

American Association of University Women (AAUW). (2001). *Hostile hallways: Bullying, teasing, and sexual harassment in school.* New York, NY: AAUW Foundation.

American Civil Liberties Union (ACLU). (2006, February 18). *ACLU hails federal court ruling on school trainings aimed at reducing anti-gay harassment.* Available at aclu. org/lgbt/youth/24215prs20060218.html

American Civil Liberties Union (ACLU). (2013a, April 4). *Texas school reverses decision to allow transgender student to wear dress to prom.* Available at www.aclu.org/lgbt-rights/texas-school-reverses-decision-and-allows-transgender-student-wear-dress-prom

American Civil Liberties Union (ACLU). (2013b, April 24). *Know your rights: Transgender people and the law.* Available at www.aclu.org/translaw

Anderson, J. D. (1997, April). Supporting the invisible minority. *Educational Leadership, 54*(7), 65–68.

Anzaldúa, G. (1990). La conciencia de la mestiza: Towards a new consciousness. In G. Anzaldúa (Ed.), *Haciendo caras: Making face, making soul* (pp. 377–389). San Francisco, CA: Aunt Lute.

Aptheker, H. (1992). *Anti-racism in U.S. history: The first two hundred years.* New York, NY: Greenwood Press.

Associated Press. (2003, August 14). Lesbian stabbing coverage draws cries of bias. Available at planetout.com/news/

Atkinson, B. (2008). Apple jumper, teacher babe, and bland uniformer teacher: Fashioning feminine teacher bodies. *Educational Studies, 44*(2), 98–121.

Baker, C. (2002). *Putting the "S" in GSA.* Available at www.glsen.or/templates/student/ section=47&record=899

Beemyn, G. (2013). The children should lead us: Diane Ehrensaft's gender born, gender made: Raising healthy gender nonconforming children. *Journal of LGBT Youth, 10*(1–2), 159–162.

Bello, N., Flynn, S., Palmer, H., Rodriguez, R., & Vente, A. (2004). *Hear me out: True stories of teens educating and confronting homophobia.* Toronto, Ontario: Second Story.

Biegel, S. (2010). *The right to be out: Sexual orientation and gender identity in America's public schools.* Minneapolis, MN: University of Minnesota Press.

Birkett, M., Espelage, D. L., & Koenig, B. (2008). LGB and questioning students in schools: The moderating effects of homophobic bullying and school climate on negative outcomes. *Journal of Youth and Adolescence, 38*, 989–1000.

Blackburn, M. V. (2004, Spring). Understanding agency beyond school-sanctioned activities. *Theory into Practice, 43*, 102–110.

Blackburn, M. V. (2005, January). Agency in borderland discourses: Examining language use in a community center with Black queer youth. *Teachers College Record, 107*, 89–113.

Blaise, M. (2005). *Play it straight: Uncovering gender discourses in the early childhood classroom.* New York, NY: Routledge.

Blanchard, D. (Counterlight). (2009, June 21). Who rioted at the Stonewall Bar that night? [Web log post]. *Counterlight's Peculiars.* Available at counterlightsrantsandblather1. blogspot.com/2009/06/who-rioted-at-stonewall-bar-that-night.html

Blount, J. (2006). *Fit to teach: Same-sex desire, gender, and school work in the twentieth century.* Albany, NY: State University of New York Press.

Bochenek, M., & Brown, A. W. (2001). *Hatred in the hallways: Violence and discrimination against lesbian, gay, bisexual, and transgender students in U.S. schools.* New York, NY: Human Rights Watch.

Boldt, G. M. (1996). Sexist and heterosexist responses to gender bending in an elementary classroom. *Curriculum Inquiry, 26*, 113–131.

Bontempo, D. E., & D'Augelli, A. R. (2002). Effects of at-school victimization and sexual orientation on lesbian, gay, or bisexual youths' health risk behavior. *Journal of Adolescent Health, 30*, 364–374.

Bornstein, K. (1994). *Gender outlaw: On men, women, and the rest of us.* New York, NY: Routledge.

Bowers v. Hardwick, 478 U.S. 186 (1986).

Britzman, D. P. (1995). Is there a queer pedagogy? Or, stop reading straight. *Educational Theory, 45*, 151–165.

Britzman, D. P. (1997). What is this thing called love? New discourses for understanding gay and lesbian youth. In S. de Castell & M. Bryson (Eds.), *Radical in(ter)ventions: Identity, politics, and difference/s in educational praxis* (pp. 183–207). Albany, NY: State University of New York Press.

Britzman, D. P., & Gilbert, J. (2004, March). What will have been said about gayness in teacher education. *Teaching Education, 15*, 81–96.

Brownmiller, S. (1970, March 15). "Sisterhood is powerful": A member of the women's liberation movement explains what it's all about. *New York Times Magazine*, p. 140.

Bryson, M., & de Castell, S. (1993). Praxis makes im/perfect. *Journal of Canadian Education, 18*, 285–305.

Bryson, M., MacIntosh, L., Jordan, S., & Lin, H. (2006). Virtually queer? Homing devices, mobility, and un/belongings. *Canadian Journal of Communication, 31*, 791–814.

Buckel, D. (1999). Gay-straight alliances and other gay-related student groups. Available at www.researchgate.net/publication/234707524_Gay-Straight_Alliances_and_

Other_Gay-Related_Student_Groups Quote is from: 130 Cong. Rec. 19211-52 (1984), Id. at 19224

Burke, D. (2013, June 28). Conservatives brace for "marriage revolution" [Web log post]. *CNN Belief Blog*. Available at religion.blogs.cnn.com/2013/06/28/conservatives-brace-for-themarriage-revolution/?hpt=hp_t1

Bury, R. (2005). *Cyberspaces of their own: Female fandoms online*. New York, NY: Peter Lang.

Capper, C. A. (1999). (Homo)sexualities, organizations, and administration: Possibilities for in(queer)y. *Educational Researcher, 28*, 4–11.

Capper, C. A., Schulte, K., & McKinney, S. A. (2009). Why school principals must stop all teasing, harassment, and bullying in schools and how they can do so. In J. W. Koschoreck & A. K. Tooms (Eds.), *Sexuality matters: Paradigms and policies for educational leaders* (pp. 123–153). Lanham, MD: Rowman & Littlefield.

Casper, V., & Schultz, S. B. (1999). *Gay parents/straight schools: Building communication and trust*. New York, NY: Teachers College Press.

Caudillo v. Lubbock Independent School District, et al. No. 03-165 (N. D. Tex. 2004).

Chambers, A. (2013, June 19). I am sorry. *Exodus International: Reaching the World in Grace & Truth*. Available at exodusinternational.org/2013/06/i-am-sorry/

Charmaraman, L., Jones, A. E., Stein, N., & Espelage, D. (2013). Is it bullying or sexual harassment? Knowledge, attitudes, and professional development experiences of middle school staff. *Journal of School Health, 83*(6), 438–444.

Chauncey, G. (1994). *Gay New York: Gender, urban culture and the making of the gay male world, 1890–1940*. Chicago, IL: University of Chicago Press.

Clark, C. T., & Blackburn, M. V. (2009). Reading LGBT-themed literature with young people: What is possible? *The English Journal, 98*(4), 25–32.

Clarke, C. L. (1981). Lesbianism: An act of resistance. In C. Moraga & G. Anzaldúa (Eds.), *This bridge called my back: Writings by radical women of color* (pp. 128–137). Watertown, MA: Persephone.

Clarke, C. L. (1983). The failure to transform: Homophobia in the Black community. In B. Smith (Ed.), *Home girls: A Black feminist anthology* (pp. 197–208). New York, NY: Kitchen Table: Woman of Color Press.

Coalition for Positive Sexuality (1996, 2008, 2013). Available at www.positive.org/

Cohen, C. (1997). Punks, bulldaggers, and welfare queens: The radical potential of queer politics. *GLQ: A Journal of Gay and Lesbian Studies, 3*(4), 437–465.

Cohen, C. (1999). *Boundaries of Blackness: AIDS and the breakdown of Black politics*. Chicago, IL: University of Chicago Press.

Colin v. Orange Unified School District, 83 F. Supp. 2d 1135 (C.D. Cal. 2000).

Combahee River Collective. (1982). A Black feminist statement. In B. Smith, P. B. Scott, & G. T. Hull (Eds.), *All the women are White, all the men are Black, but some of us are brave: Black women's studies* (pp. 13–22). Old Westbury, NY: Feminist Press.

Connell, R. W. (1987). *Gender and power: Society, the person, and sexual politics*. Palo Alto, CA: Stanford University Press.

Cory, D. W. (1951). *The homosexual in America: A subjective approach.* New York, NY: Greenberg.

Cruz, C. (2011). LGBTQ youth talk back: A meditation on resistance and witnessing. *International Journal of Qualitative Studies in Education, 24*(5), 547–558.

Cyber queers. (1996, Nov.). *Lesbian News, 22*(4).

D'Augelli, A. R., Grossman, A. H., & Starks, M. T. (2006). Childhood gender atypicality, victimization, and PTSE among lesbian, gay, and bisexual youth. *Journal of Interpersonal Violence, 21,* 1462–1482.

D'Emilio, J. (1983). *Sexual politics, sexual communities: The making of a homosexual minority in the United States, 1940–1970.* Chicago, IL: University of Chicago Press.

D'Emilio, J. (2003). *Lost prophet! The life and times of Bayard Rustin.* New York, NY: Free Press.

Davis v. Monroe County Board of Education. 526 U.S. 629 (1999).

DeHaan, S., Kuper, L. E., Magee, J. C., Bigelow, L., & Mustanski, B. S. (2013). The interplay between online and offline explorations of identity, relationships, and sex: A mixed-methods study with LGBT youth. *Journal of Sex Research, 50*(5), 421–434.

DePalma, R., & Atkinson, E. (2006). The sound of silence: Talking about sexual orientation and schooling. *Sex Education, 6*(4), 333–349.

Diamond, L. M., & Savin-Williams, R. C. (2000). Explaining diversity in the development of same-sex sexuality among young women. *Journal of Social Issues, 56*(2), 297–313.

Diaz, E. M., & Kosciw, J. G. (2009). *The experiences of lesbian, gay, bisexual, and transgender students in our nation's schools.* New York, NY: Gay, Lesbian & Straight Education Network.

Diaz-Kozlowski, T. (2013, May 2). Testimonios of a marimacha: Ethnographic tensions and resistance at the Alliance School Milwaukee. Unpublished paper presented at LGBT Research Symposium: Methodological Challenges and Opportunities, University of Illinois at Urbana-Champaign.

Driver, S. (2006). Virtually queer youth communities of girls and birls: Dialogical spaces of identity work and desiring exchanges. In D. Buckingham & R. Willett (Eds.), *Digital generations: Children, young people, and new media* (pp. 229–245). Mahwah, NJ: Erlbaum.

Driver, S. (2007). *Queer girls and popular culture: Reading, resisting, and creating media.* New York, NY: Peter Lang.

Duncan, G. A. (2005). Black youth, identity, and ethics. *Educational Theory, 55,* 3–22.

East High School PRISM Club v. Seidel. United States District Court, 95F. Supp. 2nd 1239 (2000). Available at www.leagle.com/decision-result/?xmldoc/2000133495FSupp2d1239_11228.xml/docbase/CSLWAR2-1986-2006

Ehrensaft, D. (2013). "Look, mom, I'm a boy—Don't tell anyone I was a girl." *Journal of LGBT Youth, 10*(1–2), 9–28.

Enke, A. F. (2012). Introduction: Transfeminist perspectives. In A. F. Enke (Ed.), *Transfeminist perspectives: In and beyond transgender and gender studies* (pp. 1–15). Philadelphia, PA: Temple University Press.

Erdely, S. R. (2012, February 2). One town's war on gay teens. *Rolling Stone.* Available at www.rollingstone.com/politics/news/one-towns-war-on-gay-teens-20120202

Erni, J. N. (2003). Run queer Asia run. *Journal of Homosexuality, 45*(2–4), 381–384.

Esseks, J. (2010). Victory for Constance McMillen! [Web log post]. *ACLU Bog of Rights.* Available at www.aclu.org/blog/content/victory-constance-mcmillen

Faderman, L. (1981). *Surpassing the love of men: Romantic friendship and love between women from the renaissance to the present.* New York, NY: HarperCollins.

Fann, R. Q. (2005). Growing up gay in China. In J. Sears (Ed.), *Gay, lesbian, and transgender issues in education: Programs, policies, and practices* (pp. 37–44). New York, NY: Harrington Park Press.

Ferfolja, T., & Robinson, K. H. (2004). Why anti-homophobia education in teacher education? Perspectives from Australian teacher educators. *Teaching Education, 15*(1), 9–27.

Flecker, M., & Gutteridge, L. (2008). Gay positive literature in libraries could save lives: The leadership role for teacher–librarians in social justice issues. *Teaching Librarian, 15*(2), 38–39.

Focus on the Family. (2013). *Day of dialogue.* Available at www.dayofdialogue.com/

Foote, S. (2005). Deviant classics: Pulps and the making of lesbian print culture. *Signs: Journal of Women in Culture and Society, 31*(1), 169–190.

Foucault, M. (1980). *History of sexuality, Vol. 1. An Introduction.* New York, NY: Vintage.

Franke, K. M. (2004). The domesticated liberty of *Lawrence v. Texas. Columbia Law Review, 104*(5), 1399–1426.

Fraser, V. (2010). Queer closets and rainbow hyperlinks: The construction and constraint of queer subjectivities online. *Sexuality Research and Social Policy, 7*(1), 30–36.

Fricke v. Lynch, 491 F.Supp. 381 (1980).

Friend, R. A. (1995). Choices, not closets: Heterosexism and homophobia in schools. In L. Weis & M. Fine (Eds.), *Beyond silenced voices: Class, race, and gender in United States schools* (pp. 209–235). Albany, NY: State University of New York Press.

Frye, P. R. (2002). Facing discrimination, organizing for freedom: The transgender community. In J. D'Emilio, W. B. Turner, & U. Vaid (Eds.), *Creating change: Sexuality, public policy, and civil rights* (pp. 451–468). New York, NY: Stonewall Inn Editions.

Galarte, F. J. (2012, October 10). Siempre en mi mente: On trans*violence. *The Feminist Wire.* Available at thefeministwire.com/2012/10/siempre-en-mi-mente-on-trans-violence/

Gay, Lesbian & Straight Education Network (GLSEN). (2013a). Background and information about gay-straight alliances. Available at http://glsen-cloud.mediapolis.com/cgi-bin/iowa/all/library/record/2336.html

GLSEN, Center for Innovative Public Health Research, and Crimes Against Children Research Center. (2013b). *Out online: The experiences of Lesbian, Gay, Bisexual and Transgender youth on the Internet.* New York, NY: GLSEN.

Gender Public Advocacy Coalition (GenderPAC). (2002). *Gender PAC annual report 2002.* Washington, DC: Author.

Gilgoff, D. (2010, October 6). Christian group pulls support for event challenging homosexuality [Web log post]. *CNN Belief Blog.* Available at religion.blogs. cnn.com/2010/10/06/christian-group-pulls-support-for-event-challenging-homosexuality/?hpt=T2

Gillman v. School Board of Holmes County, 5:08-cv-34 (N. D. Fla. 2008).

Goode, E. (2013, July 2). Ruling might also ease the way for same-sex divorces. *New York Times.* Available at www.nyt.com/2013/07/03/us/ruling-might-also-ease-the-way-for-same-sex-divorces.html?hp&_r=0

Goodridge v. Dept. of Public Health, 798 N.E.2d 941 (Mass. 2003).

Graves, K. (2009). *And they were wonderful teachers: Florida's purge of gay and lesbian teachers.* Urbana, IL: University of Illinois Press.

Gray, M. L. (2007). From websites to Walmart: Youth, identity work, and the queering of boundary publics in Small Town, USA. *American Studies, 48*(2), 49–59.

Greytak, E. A., Kosciw, J. G., & Boesen, M. J. (2013). Putting the "T" in "Resource": The benefits of LGBT-related school resources for transgender youth. *Journal of LGBT Youth, 10*(1–12), 45–163.

Grossman, A. H., & D'Augelli, A. R. (2006). Transgender youth: Invisible and vulnerable. *Journal of Homosexuality, 51,* 111–128.

Gruber, J. E., & Fineran, S. (2008). Comparing the impact of bullying and sexual harassment victimization on the mental and physical health of adolescents. *Sex Roles, 59*(1–2), 1–13.

Gutiérrez, R. (2002). Enabling the practices of mathematics teachers in context: Toward a new equity research agenda. *Mathematical Thinking and Learning, 42*(2–3), 145–187.

Gutstein, E. (2003). Teaching and learning mathematics for social justice in an urban, Latino school. *Journal for Research in Mathematics Education, 34*(1), 37–73.

Hackford-Peer, K. (2010). In the name of safety: Discursive positionings of queer youth. *Studies in Philosophy and Education, 29*(6), 541–556.

Hargittai, E. (2011). Open doors, closed spaces? Differentiated adoption of social network sites by user background. In P. Chow-White & L. Nakamura (Eds.), *Race After the Internet* (pp. 223–245). New York, NY: Routledge.

Harp, D., Bachman, I., Rosas-Moreno, T. C., & Loke, J. (2010). Wave of hope: African American youth use media and engage more civically, politically than Whites. *Howard Journal of Communication, 21,* 224–246.

Heck, N. C., Flentje, A., & Cochran, B. N. (2011). Offsetting risk: High school gay-straight alliances and lesbian, gay, bisexual, and transgender youth. *School Psychology Quarterly, 26*(2), 161–174.

Helfand, G. (1996, November 12). Queer frontier. *The advocate* (720).

Hillier, L., & Harrison, L. (2007). Building realities less limited than their own: Young people practicing same-sex attraction on the Internet. *Sexualities, 10*(1), 82–100.

Hillier, L., Mitchell, K. J., & Ybarra, M. L. (2012). The Internet as a safety net: Findings from a series of online focus groups with LGB and non-LGB young people in the United States. *Journal of LGBT Youth, 9*, 225–246.

Hollingsworth v. Perry, 570 U.S.__ (2013).

Holman, E. G., & Oswald, R. F. (2011). Nonmetropolitan GLBTQ families: When and where does their sexuality matter? *Journal of GLBT Family Studies, 7*, 436–456.

Horne, T. (2001, Oct. 30). Gay-Straight Alliance sues high school. *Indianapolis Star.*

Human Rights Campaign. (2013). Employment Non-Discrimination Act. Available at http://www.hrc.org/laws-and-legislation/federal-legislation/employment-non-discrimination-act

Humm, A. (1994). *Re-building the "Rainbow": The holy war over inclusion in New York City.* Unpublished manuscript.

Hyland, N. E. (2010). Intersections of race and sexuality in a teacher education course. *Teaching Education, 21*(4), 385–401.

Irvine, J. (Ed.). (1994). *Sexual cultures and the construction of adolescent identities.* Philadelphia, PA: Temple University Press.

It Gets Better Project. (2010–2013). *It Gets Better Project* [Website]. Available at www.itgetsbetter.org

Ito, M., Davidson, C., Jenkins, H., Lee, C., Eisenberg, M., & Weiss, J. (2008). Foreword. In D. Buckingham (Ed.), *Youth, identity, and digital media* (pp. vii–ix). Cambridge, MA: MIT Press.

Jacobs, S. (2013). Creating safe and welcoming schools for LGBT students: Ethical and legal issues. *Journal of School Violence, 12*(1), 98–115.

Jenkins, C. A. (1993). Young adult novels with gay/lesbian characters and themes, 1969–1982: A historical reading of content, gender, and narrative distance. *Journal of Youth Services in Libraries, 7*, 43–55.

Johnson, D. K. (2006). *The lavender scare: The cold war persecution of gays and lesbians in the federal government.* Chicago, IL: University of Chicago Press.

Johnson, E. P., & Henderson, M. G. (Eds.). (2005). *Black queer studies: A critical anthology.* Durham, NC: Duke University Press.

Jordan, M. D. (1998). *The invention of sodomy in Christian theology.* Chicago, IL: University of Chicago Press.

Katz, J. (2007). *The invention of heterosexuality.* Chicago, IL: University of Chicago Press.

Kendall, N. (2013). *The sex education debates.* Chicago, IL: University of Chicago Press.

Kilman, C. (2012, Spring). Class outing. *Teaching Tolerance, 41.* Available at www.tolerance.org/class-outing-story

Kilman, C. (2007, Spring). 'This is why we need a GSA.' *Teaching Tolerance, 31.* Available at www.tolerance.org/magazine/number-31-spring-2007/feature/why-we-need-gsa

Kimmel, M. (2010). *Misframing men: The politics of contemporary masculinities.* Piscataway, NJ: Rutgers University Press.

Kinsey, A., Pomeroy, W. B., & Martin, C. E. (1948). *Sexual behavior in the human male.* Philadelphia, PA: W. B. Saunders.

Kinsey, A., Pomeroy, W. B., Martin, C. E., & Gebhard, P. H. (1953). *Sexual behavior in the human female.* Philadelphia, PA: W. B. Saunders.

Kosciw, J. G., & Diaz, E. M. (2005). *The 2005 national school climate survey.* New York, NY: Gay, Lesbian & Straight Education Network.

Kosciw, J. G., & Diaz, E. M. (2008). *Involved, invisible, and ignored: The experiences of lesbian, gay, bisexual, and transgender parents and their children in our nation's K–12 schools.* New York, NY: Gay, Lesbian & Straight Education Network.

Kosciw, J. G., Diaz, E. M., & Greytak, E. A. (2007). *The 2007 national school climate survey: The experiences of lesbian, gay, bisexual, and transgender youth in our nation's schools.* New York, NY: Gay, Lesbian & Straight Education Network.

Kosciw, J. G., Greytak, E. A., Bartkiewicz, M. J., Boesen, M. J., & Palmer, N. A. (2012). *The 2011 national school climate survey: The experiences of lesbian, gay, bisexual, and transgender youth in our nation's schools.* New York, NY: Gay, Lesbian & Straight Education Network.

Kosciw, J. G., Greytak, E. A., Diaz, E. M., & Bartkiewicz, M. J. (2010). *The 2009 national school climate survey: The experiences of lesbian, gay, bisexual, and transgender youth in our nation's schools.* New York, NY: Gay, Lesbian & Straight Education Network.

Kraft-Ebbing, R. (1947). *Psychopathia sexualis; a medico-forensic study.* New York, NY: Pioneer.

Kumashiro, K. (2001). *Troubling intersections of race and sexuality: Queer students of color and anti-oppressive education.* Lanham, MD: Rowman & Littlefield.

Kumashiro, K. (2002). *Troubling education: Queer activism and anti-oppressive education.* New York, NY: Routledge.

Kumashiro, K. (2003). Queer ideas in education. *Journal of Homosexuality, 45*(2/3/4), 365–367.

Kumashiro, K. (2004). Uncertain beginnings: Learning to teach paradoxically. *Theory into Practice, 43*(2), 111–115.

Lambda Legal. (2008). *Out, safe, & respected: Your rights at school.* Available at www.lambdalegal.org/publications/out-safe-respected

Landau, J. (2003, June 23). Ripple effect: Sodomy statutes as weapons. *The Nation,* 13–16.

Lau, H. (2007). Pluralism: A principle for children's rights. *Harvard Civil Rights–Civil Liberties Law Review, 42*(2), 317–372.

Lawrence v. Texas, 539 U.S. 558 (2003).

Leck, G. M. (2000). Heterosexual or homosexual? Reconsidering binary narratives on sexual identities in urban schools. *Education and Urban Society, 32,* 324–348.

Lee, C. (2002). The impact of belonging to a high school gay/straight alliance. *The High School Journal, 85*(3), 13–26.

Lee, N., Murphy, D., North, L., & Ucelli, J. (2000). Bridging race, class, and sexuality for school reform. In J. D'Emilio, W. B. Turner, & U. Vaid (Eds.), *Creating change:*

Sexuality, public policy, and civil rights (pp. 251–260). New York, NY: St. Martin's Press.

Lemon v. Kurtzman, 403 U.S. 602 (1971).

Lichty, L., Torres, J., Valenti, M., & Buchanan, N. (2008). Sexual harassment policies in K–12 schools: Examining accessibility to students and content. *Journal of School Health, 78*(11), 607–614.

Lipton, M. (2008). Queer readings of popular culture: Searching [to] out the subtext. In Susan Driver (Ed.), *Queer youth cultures* (pp. 163–177), Albany, NY: State University of New York Press.

Lofquist, D. (2012, May). Same-sex couples' consistency in reports of marital status. Paper presented at the annual meeting of the Population Association of America, San Francisco, CA. Available at www.census.gov/hhes/samesex/files/Lofquist.PAA. paper.pdf

Logue, J. (2008). The unbelievable truth and the dilemmas of ignorance. *Philosophy of Education,* 54–62.

Lorde, A. (1984). *Sister/outsider: Essays and speeches.* Trumansburg, NY: Crossing.

Lorde, A. (1988). *A burst of light: Essays by Audre Lorde.* Ithaca, NY: Firebrand.

Loutzenheiser, L. W., & MacIntosh, L. B. (2004, Spring). Citizenships, sexualities, and education. *Theory Into Practice, 43,* 151–158.

Love, B. L. (2012). *Hip Hop's li'l sistas speak: Negotiating Hip Hop identities and politics in the New South.* New York, NY: Peter Lang.

Lugg, C. A. (2003). Sissies, faggots, lezzies, and dykes: Gender, sexual orientation, and a new politics of education? *Educational Administration Quarterly, 39,* 95–137.

Lui, R. (2011, June 18). Boy punished for wearing dress to school [Video]. MSNBC. Retrieved June 15, 2013 from video.msnbc.msn.com/msnbc/43450517#43450517

MacIntosh, L., & Bryson, M. (2008). Youth, MySpace, and the interstitial spaces of becoming and belonging. *Journal of LGBT Youth, 5*(1), 133–142.

Manalansan, M. (2003). *Global divas: Filipino men in the diaspora.* Durham, NC: Duke University Press.

Martino, W., & Cumming-Potvin, W. (2011). "They didn't have out there gay parents— They just looked like normal regular parents": Investigating teachers' approaches to addressing same-sex parenting and non-normative sexuality in the elementary school classroom. *Curriculum Inquiry, 41*(4), 480–501.

Mayo, C. (2004a). *Disputing the subject of sex: Sexuality and public school controversies.* Lanham, MD: Rowman & Littlefield.

Mayo, C. (2004b). The tolerance that dare not speak its name. In M. Boler (Ed.), *Democratic dialogue in education: Disturbing silence, troubling speech* (pp. 33–47). New York, NY: Peter Lang.

Mayo, C. (2007). Intermittently queer. In N. Rodriguez & W. Pinar (Eds.), *Queering straight teachers: Discourse and identity in education* (pp. 182–199). New York, NY: Peter Lang.

Mayo, C. (2008). Obscene associations: Gay-Straight Alliances, the Equal Access Act, and abstinence-only policy. *Sexuality Research and Social Policy, 5*(2), 45–55.

Mayo, C. (2011). Sexuality education policy and the educative potentials of risk and rights. *Policy Futures in Education, 9*(3), 406–415.

Mayo, C. (forthcoming). Unsettled relations: Schools, gay marriage, and educating for sexuality. *Educational Theory.*

Mayo, J. B. (2013). Critical pedagogy enacted in the Gay-Straight Alliance: New possibilities for a third space in teacher development. *Educational Researcher, 42*(5), 266–275.

McCready, L. T. (2010). *Making space for diverse masculinities: Difference, intersectionality, and engagement in an urban high school.* New York, NY: Peter Lang.

McGuire, J. K., Anderson, C. R., Toomey, R. B., & Russell, S. (2010). School climate for transgender youth: A mixed method investigation of student experiences and school responses. *Journal of Youth and Adolescence, 39*, 1175–1188.

McKenzie, K. B., Christman, D. E., Hernandez, F., Fierro, E., Capper, C. A., Dantley, M., . . . Scheurich, J. J. (2008). From the field: A proposal for educating leaders for social justice. *Educational Administration Quarterly, 44*(1), 111–138.

Mehta, C. M., & Strough, J. (2010). Gender segregation and gender-typing in adolescence. *Sex Roles, 63*, 251–263.

Meyer, E. (2008). Gendered harassment in secondary schools: Understanding teachers' (non)interventions. *Gender and Education, 20*(6), 555–570.

Miceli, M. (2005). *Standing out, standing together.* New York, NY: Routledge.

Mossberger, K., Tolbert, C. J., & Gilbert, M. (2006). Race, place, and information technology. *Urban Affairs Review, 41*(5), 583–620.

Mouw, T., & Entwisle, B. (2006). Residential segregation and interracial friendship in schools. *American Journal of Sociology, 112*(2), 394–441.

Mustanski, B., Lyons, T., & Garcia, S. (2011). Internet use and sexual health of young men who have sex with men. *Health Psychology, 30*, 597–605.

Nabozny v. Podlesny, 92 F.3d 446 (7th Cir. 1996).

Nakamura, L. (2000). Race in/for cyberspace: Identity tourism and racial passing on the internet. In D. Bell & B. M. Kennedy (Eds.), *The cybercultures reader* (pp. 712–722). New York, NY: Routledge.

Namaste, V. (2009). Undoing theory: The "transgender question" and the epistemic violence of Anglo-American feminist theory. *Hypatia, 24*(3), 11–32.

National Education Association. (1975). *Code of ethics.* Available at www.nea.org/home/30442.htm

New York City Board of Education. (1994). *Comprehensive instructional program first grade teachers' resource guide review draft. (Children of the Rainbow).* New York, NY: Board of Education Publications.

Newton, H. (1973). A letter from Huey. In L. Richmond & G. Noguera (Eds.), *The gay liberation book: Writings and photographs on gay (men's) liberation* (pp. 142–145). San Francisco: Ramparts.

Nguon v. Wolf, 517 F. Supp. 2d 1177 (Dist. Court, CD California, 2007).

Nip, J. Y. M. (2004). The relationship of online and offline communities: The case of the Queer Sisters. *Media, Culture, and Society, 26*, 409–420.

Oncale v. Sundowner Offshore Services, Inc. 83 F.3d 118 (1998).

O'Shaughnessy, M., Russell, S., Heck, K., Calhoun, C., & Laub, C. (2004). *Safe place to learn: Consequences of harassment based on actual or perceived sexual orientation and gender non-conformity and steps for making schools safer*. San Francisco, CA: California Safe Schools Coalition.

Oswald, R. F., & Culton, L. S. (2003). Under the rainbow: Rural gay life and its relevance for family providers. *Family Relations, 52*, 72–81.

Paceley, M. S., & Flynn, K. (2012). Media representations of bullying toward queer youth: Gender, race, and age discrepancies. *Journal of LGBT Youth, 9*(4), 340–356.

Paradise, E. (2008, March 26). LGBTIQQ youth and online environments: A mixed methods approach. Paper presented at the annual meeting of the American Educational Research Association, New York, NY.

Parker v. Hurley, C. A. 474, F. Supp. 2d 261 (D. Mass. 2007).

Parrish, M. (2002). *The "S" in GSA: Not just lip service*. New York, NY: Gay, Lesbian & Straight Education Network. Available at www.glsen.org/templates/students/ section=47&record=1388

Pascoe, C. J. (2007). *Dude, you're a fag: Masculinity and sexuality in high school*. Berkeley: University of California Press.

Payne, E., & Smith, M. (2012). Rethinking "safe schools" approaches for LGBTQ students: Changing the questions we ask. *Perspectives in Multicultural Education, 14*(4), 187–193.

Peiss, C. (1986). *Cheap amusements: Women and leisure in turn-of-the-century New York*. Philadelphia, PA: Temple University Press.

Perrotti, J., & Westheimer, K. (2001). *When the drama club is not enough: Lessons from the safe schools program for gay and lesbian students*. Boston, MA: Beacon Press.

Pharr, S. (1997). *Homophobia: A weapon of sexism*. Hoboken, NJ: Chardon.

Poteat, V. P., & Espelage, D. L. (2007). Predicting psychosocial consequences of homophobic victimization in middle school students. *Journal of Early Adolescence, 27*(2), 175–191.

Poteat, V. P., Espelage, D. L., & Koenig, B. W. (2009). Willingness to remain friends and attend school with lesbian and gay peers: Relational expressions of prejudice among heterosexual youth. *Journal of Youth and Adolescence, 38*, 952–962.

Preston, J. (2013, June 30). Gay married man in Florida is approved for green card. *New York Times*. Available at www.nytimes.com/2013/07/01/us/gay-married-man-in-florida-is-approved-for-green-card.html?_r=0

Quillian, L., & Campbell, M. (2001, August). Segregation forever? Racial composition and multiracial friendship segregation in American schools. Paper presented at the annual meeting of the American Sociological Association, Anaheim, CA.

Radicalesbians. (1970). The woman identified woman. *Come Out!*, *4*. Available at www. queerrhetoric.com/2011/04/03/the-woman-identified-woman/

Rands, K. (2013). Supporting transgender and gender nonconforming youth through teaching mathematics for social justice. *Journal of LGBT Youth, 10*(1–2), 106–126.

Rasmus, T. (2013, June 12). Free to be you and me? Boy punished for wearing makeup to school. Available at www.refinery29.com/2013/06/48351/boys-wearing-makeup-dress-code

Rasmussen, M. L. (2004). The problem of coming out. *Theory into Practice, 43*, 144–150.

Rhodes, J. (2004). Homo origo: The queertext manifesto. *Computers and Composition, 21*(3), 385–388.

Rich, A. (1980). Compulsory heterosexuality and lesbian existence. *Signs, 5*(4), 631–660.

Robinson, J. P., & Espelage, D. L. (2012). Bullying explains only part of the LGBTQ-heterosexual risk disparities: Implications for policy and practice. *Educational Researcher, 41*(8), 309–319.

Robinson, J. P., Espelage, D. L., & Rivers, I. (2013). Developmental trends in peer victimization and emotional distress in LGB and heterosexual youth. *Pediatrics, 131*(3), 423–430.

Rochlin, M. (1972). The heterosexual questionnaire. In M. S. Kimmel & M. A. Messner (Eds.), *Men's Lives* (4th ed., p. 472). Boston, MA: Allyn & Bacon.

Rodriguez, N. (2007). Just queer it. In N. S. Rodriguez & W. F. Pinar (Eds.), *Queering straight teachers: Discourse and identity in education* (pp. vii–xiii). New York, NY: Peter Lang.

Rofes, E. (2005). *Status quo v. status queer: A radical rethinking of sexuality and schooling.* Lanham, MD: Rowman & Littlefield.

Ross, M. B. (2005). Beyond the closet as raceless paradigm. In E. P. Johnson & M. G. Henderson (Eds.), *Black queer studies: A critical anthology* (pp. 161–189). Durham, NC: Duke University Press.

Ruenzel, D. (1999). Pride and prejudice. *Teacher Magazine, 10*(7), 22–27.

Russell, S. T. (2002). Queer in America: Citizenship for sexual minority youth. *Applied Developmental Science, 6*(4), 258–263.

Ryabov, I. (2011). Adolescent academic outcomes in school context: Network effects reexamined. *Journal of Adolescence, 34*, 915–927.

Ryan, C. C., Huebner, D., Diaz, R., & Sanchez, J. (2009). Family rejection as a predictor of negative health outcomes in White and Latino lesbian, gay, and bisexual young adults. *Pediatrics, 123*(1), 346.

Ryan, C. L., Patraw, J. M., & Bednar, M. (2013). Discussing princess boys and pregnant men: Teaching about gender diversity and transgender experiences within elementary school curriculum. *Journal of LGBT Youth, 10*(1–2), 83–105.

Sahli, N. (1979). Smashing: Women's relationships before the fall. *Chrysalis, 8*, 17–27.

Saillant, C. (2008a, February 17). 1,000 march in Oxnard in tribute to slain teen. *Los Angeles Times*. Available at www.larticles.latimes.com/2008/feb/17/local/me-oxnard17

Saillant, C. (2008b, May 8). Lawyer blames school in shooting of gay Oxnard student. *Los Angeles Times*. Available at www.latimes.com/news/printedition/california/la-me-oxnard8-2008may08,0,6901056.story

Sears, J. T. (1992). Educators, homosexuality, and homosexual students: Are personal feelings related to professional beliefs? *Journal of Homosexuality, 22*(3–4), 29–80.

Sears, J. T. (1995). Black-gay or gay-Black? Choosing identities and identifying choices. In G. Unks (Ed.), *The gay teen* (pp. 135–157). New York, NY: Routledge.

Sedgwick, E. K. (1990). *Epistemology of the closet*. Berkeley, CA: University of California Press.

Sieczkowski, C. (2013, June 11). Parents of boy chastised for wearing make up to school call for tolerance. *Huffington Post*. Available at www.huffingtonpost.com/2013/06/11/boy-makeup-dress-code_n_3421710.html

Silin, J. G. (1995). *Sex, death, and the education of children: Our passion for ignorance in the age of AIDS*. New York, NY: Teachers College Press.

Sleeter, C. E. (1994). A multicultural educator views White racism. *Education Digest, 59*(9), 33–36.

Slesaransky-Poe, G., Ruzzi, L., Dimedio, C., & Stanley, J. (2013). Is this the right elementary school for my gender nonconforming child? *Journal of LGBT Youth, 10*(1–2), 29–44.

Smith, B. (1983). Introduction. In B. Smith (Ed.), *Home girls: A Black feminist anthology* (pp. xix–lvi). New York, NY: Kitchen Table: Woman of Color Press.

Smith-Rosenberg, C. (1975). The female world of love and ritual: Relations between women in nineteenth-century America. *Signs, 1*(1), 1–29.

Smothers, R. (2004, May 12). Newark preaches tolerance of gays year after killing. *New York Times*, B5. Available at www.nytimes.com/2004/05/12/nyregion/newark-preaches-tolerance-of-gays-year-after-killing.html

Sonnie, A. (Ed.). (2000). *Revolutionary voices: A multicultural queer youth anthology*. Los Angeles, CA: Alyson Books.

Stein, N. (2003). Bullying or sexual harassment? The missing discourse of rights in an era of zero tolerance. *Arizona Law Review, 45*(3), 783–799.

Stengel, B. (2010). The complex case of fear and safe space. *Studies in Philosophy and Education, 29*, 523–540.

Stengel, B., & Weems, L. (2010). Questioning safe spaces: An introduction. *Studies in Philosophy and Education, 29*, 505–507.

Steph. (2013). The day that DOMA died [Web log post]. *All For the Love of You: A Chronicle of Suburban Southern Life*. Available at www.allfortheloveofyou.com/the-day-that-doma-died/

Stone, A. R. (1995). *The war of desire and technology at the close of the mechanical age*. Cambridge, MA: MIT Press.

Stryker, S. (2008). Transgender history, homonormativity, and disciplinarity. *Radical History Review, 2008*(100), 145–157.

Sykes, H. (2004). Pedagogies of censorship, injury, and masochism: Teacher responses to homophobic speech in physical education. *Curriculum Studies, 36*(1), 75–99.

Talburt, S. (2004). Constructions of LGBT youth: Opening up subject positions. *Theory into Practice, 43*(2), 116–121.

Texas GSA Network. (2011). Update: Flour Bluff GSA approved by ISD. Available at texasgsa.org/news-archive/109-update-flour-bluff-gsa-approved-by-isd

Thompson, I. (2010). Miss McMillen goes to Washington! [Web log post]. ACLU Blog of Rights. Available at www.aclu.org/blog/lgbt-rights/ms-mcmillen-goes-washington

Thorne, B. (1993). *Gender play: Girls and boys at school.* New Brunswick, NJ: Rutgers University Press.

Tinker v. Des Moines Independent Community School District, 393 U. S. 503 (1969).

Tolman, D. (2006). In a different position: Conceptualizing female adolescent development within compulsory heterosexuality. *New Directions for Child and Adolescent Development, 112,* 71–89.

Toomey, R. B., McGuire, J. K., & Russell, S. T. (2012). Heteronormativity, school climates, and perceived safety for gender nonconforming peers. *Journal of Adolescence, 35,* 187–196.

Trotter, A. (2006, September 13). Minorities still face digital divide. *Education Week, 26*(3), 14.

Turkle, S. (1997). Multiple subjectivity and virtual community at the end of the Freudian century. *Sociological Inquiry, 67*(1), 72–84.

Tynes, B., Reynolds, L., & Greenfield, P. M. (2004). Adolescence, race, and ethnicity on the Internet: A comparison of discourse in monitored vs. unmonitored chat rooms. *Journal of Applied Psychology, 25,* 667–684.

Ueno, K., Wright, E. R., Gayman, M. D., & McCabe, J. M. (March, 2012). Segregation in gay, lesbian and bisexual youth's personal networks: Testing structural constraint, choice homophily and compartmentalization hypotheses. *Social Forces, 90*(3), 971–991.

United States Congress (1972). Title IX of the Education Amendments of 1972, 20 U.S.C. §1681, §1687.

United States Congress (98th). (1984). Equal Access Act (EAA). 20 U.S.C. § 4071, Available at www.law.cornell.edu/uscode/text/20/4071

United States v. Windsor, 570 U.S.__(2013).

Weeks, J. (1990). *Sexuality and its discontents: Meanings, myths, and modern sexualities.* New York, NY: Routledge.

Weems, L. (2010). From "home" to "camp": Theorizing the space of safety. *Studies in Philosophy and Education, 29,* 557–568.

Wells, G. (2011). Making room for daddies: Male couples creating families through adoption. *Journal of GLBT Family Studies, 7*(1–2), 155–181.

Welsh, M. (2011). Growing up in a same-sex parented family: The adolescent voice of experience. *Journal of GLBT Family Studies, 7*(1–2), 49–71.

White, D., & Stephenson, R. (2013). Identity formation, outness, and sexual risk among gay and bisexual men. *American Journal of Men's Health, 20*(10), 1–12.

Widmar v. Vincent, 454 U.S. 263 (1981).

Williams, T., Connolly, J., Pepler, D., & Craig, W. (2005). Peer victimization, social support, and psychosocial adjustment of sexual minority adolescents. *Journal of Youth and Adolescence, 34*, 471–482.

Wilson, A. (1996). How we find ourselves: Identity development and two-spirit people. *Harvard Educational Review, 66*, 303–317.

Wittman, C. (1970). Refugees from Amerika: A gay manifesto. *Gay Flames pamphlet no. 9.* Available at www.queerrhetoric.com/2011/04/02/refugees-from-amerika-a-gay-manifesto/

Wooledge, S. (2012, March 11). Major victory in Anoka-Hennepin school district bullying lawsuit. *Daily Kos.* Available at www.dailykos.com/story/2012/03/11/1072927/-Major-victory-in-Anoka-Hennepin-school-district-bullying-lawsuit

Wyatt, T. J., Oswalt, S. B., White, C., & Peterson, F. L. (2008, Spring). Are tomorrow's teachers ready to deal with diverse students? Teacher candidates' attitudes toward gay men and lesbians. *Teacher Education Quarterly, 35*(2), 171–185.

Ybarra, M., & Suman, M. (2008). Reasons, assessments, and actions taken: Sex and age differences in uses of Internet health information. *Health Education Research, 23*(3), 512–521.

Yon-Leau, C., & Muñoz-Laboy, M. (2010). "I don't like to say that I'm anything": Sexuality politics and cultural critique among sexual-minority Latino youth. *Sexuality research and social policy, 7*, 105–117.

Index

indigenous cultures, sexuality within, 40
institutional disrespect, response to, 37
institutionalized heteronormativity, 14
insults, 52
intentional community, 106–108
intermarriage, racial, 43
intersex people, 21
intervention, school, 54, 59, 61–62, 78
Irvine, J., 40
"It Gets Better Project," 56
Ito, M., 113

Jacobs, S., 8
Jenkins, C. A., 78
Jenkins, H., 113
job protection, 10
Johnson, D. K., 23
Johnson, E. P., 40
Johnson, Marsha P. (activist), 27
Jones, A. E., 58
Jordan, Mark D., 81–82
Jordan, S., 113

Katz, J., 30, 31
Kendall, Nancy, 75
Kertbeny, Karoly, 30
Kilman, Carrie, 8, 67, 96
Kimmel, M., 43
King, Warren (student), 54
King and King (children's book), 63–64
Kinsey, Alfred, 23
Kinsey Report, 23
Kinsey scale, 23
Koenig, B., 22, 59, 88
Kosciw, J. G., 2, 45, 47, 51, 52, 53, 56, 61
Kraft-Ebbing, R., 31
Kumashiro, K., 27, 40, 69
Kuper, L. E., 108

The Ladder, 25
Lambda Legal, 11
Landau, J., 65
Latino youth, 53, 55, 98
Lau, Holning, 13
Laub, C., 6
lavender menace, 27
Lavender Scare, 23, 32
Lawrence v. Texas (2003), 65, 93
laws and policies
  on bullying, 58
  for extracurricular groups, 87–94
  for gender identity, 6
  implementing, 8–9, 33
  learning from, 7, 10, 59
  misunderstandings of, 58, 61
  oppression through, 48, 60–61, 84
  prohibiting discrimination, 6
  resource access to, 8
  for same-sex marriage, 5, 6, 62
  school-based, 7
  and school implementation, disconnect between, 59–60
  sexual orientation addressed through, 32–33
leadership practice, 15
learning
  for ethical relations, 83–86
  and sexuality, 31–32, 88
Leck, G. M., 40
Lee, C., 89, 113
Lee, N., 32
Lemon v. Kurtzman's (1971), 91
lesbian, concept of, 20
lesbian feminists, 22–23
"Lesbian Stabbing" incident, 55
LGBTQ media, beginnings of, 25–26
LGBTQ movements
  groups organizing within, 20
  histories of, 22–31

About the Author

Cris Mayo is professor and associate head in the Department of Education Policy, Organization, and Leadership Studies and professor in the Department of Gender and Women's Studies at the University of Illinois at Urbana-Champaign. Her publications in queer studies, gender and sexuality studies, and philosophy of education include *Disputing the Subject of Sex: Sexuality and Public School Controversies* (Rowman and Littlefield, 2004/2007) as well as articles in *Educational Theory, Studies in Philosophy and Education, Policy Futures in Education, Review of Research in Education*, and *Sexuality Research and Social Policy*.